Peace and Power

A Handbook of Feminist Process

Peace and Power
A Handbook of Feminist Process
Third Edition

Charlene Eldridge Wheeler
Peggy L. Chinn

Pub. No. 15-2404

National League for Nursing Press • New York

ISBN 0-88737-520-0

The cover design combines symbols of feminist concepts of Peace and Power. The hands held with the thumbs and first fingers touching are an international sign of women's unified commitment to peace within the universe. The labrys is a symbol of independent female power from ancient Crete now adopted by modern feminists. These two symbols combined reflect synergistic movement toward feminist activism. The cover was designed by Charlene Eldridge Wheeler.

This book was set in Garamond and Baskerville by Publications Development Company. Automated Graphic Systems was the printer and binder.

Printed in the United States of America

Table of Contents

Acknowledgments   vii

Prologue   xi

1. What It's All About: PEACE   1

2. How We Get There from Here: POWER   7

3. Doing It: Making the Commitment   13

4. What We Are All About: Principles of Unity   19

5. Getting Things Going: Everybody Does It   29

6. Turning It Over: Rotating Chair   37

7. Letting It Happen: Consensus   47

8. Stepping from Here to There: Closing   51

9. Valuing Diversity and Unity: Conflict Transformation   67

10. Period Pieces   83

11. Classrooms, Committees, and Institutional Constraints   89

Notes   97

About the Authors   106

Acknowledgments

We enjoy a large circle of friends and companions as we continue on our journey toward a feminist future. Many individuals have made it possible for us to share the ideas of *Peace and Power*. We have not specifically named each individual here, but we appreciate each and every one and trust that our journey together will grow and develop in the years to come.

Wilma Scott Heide, a dear friend and courageous women's movement leader of the early 1970s, gave us the inspiration and determination to venture into publishing the first edition of *Peace and Power* at Margaretdaughters, Inc.[1] She told us that when she first read the book, she wept, both from the joy of seeing feminist ideas presented in this way, and from the anguish of not having had the benefit of some of these insights in her early years of activist work. As we conveyed to her many times before her death in 1984, it is because of her own courageous living, and that of women like her, that we have been able to do the work on which these ideas are built.

Patricia Moccia, a woman of vision in our own generation, believed in the possibilities of this process for a wider circle, and initiated and facilitated the publication of the second edition by the National League for Nursing. This occurred at a time of great crisis in the health care system and at a time of dramatic change for nurses and nursing. As incongruous as it may seem to many, this book is possible in part because of our backgrounds as nurses, and the heritage we carry from many radical nurses, sometimes not-yet-feminists, who lived and worked over the last century.

Sally Barhydt, Managing Editor at the National League for Nursing, has worked with us closely during the preparation of both the second and the third editions. Her enthusiasm and support for having this book published by the League has been central to making this possible.

The groups in which we have worked have been fundamentally important in providing the opportunities to live our values, and to explore new ways of putting our values into action. These groups, and individuals in them who have contributed in particular ways to the emergence of our own thinking, include the following.

The Emma Collective was a group of women who owned a women's bookstore, now located at 168 Elmwood Avenue in Buffalo, New York. Lisa Albrecht, now at the University of Minnesota and a leader in the National Women's Studies Association, was a member of the Emma Collective at the time that we joined, and worked attentively with us as we first began to develop the insights that made this book possible. The Emma Collective used a form of rotating chair and as we worked to put language to the process, provided invaluable insights and learning experiences.

The Women's Studies Program at the State University of New York at Buffalo has a tradition since the late 1960s of using a rotating chair process in their meetings and class gatherings. We have learned from them and from many individual women who participated in the Women's Studies classes and gatherings over the years.

Various coalitions of women in the Buffalo community, including the Voices of Women Writers Coalition (1982) and International Women's Day (IWD) Coalitions (1982–1986), have provided experience and insights that have contributed to many of these ideas. In 1983, the IWD Coalition invited Wilma Scott Heide to speak at our celebration, making possible the important connection we formed with Wilma.

Cassandra: Radical Feminist Nurses Network (P.O. Box 181039, Cleveland, Ohio 44118-1039) is a network of nurses formed in 1982, committed to developing feminist analyses of issues in nursing and women's health. Our gatherings, as well as our struggles to work together across long distances to carry out responsibilities for the *NewsJournal* and the Webstership list, have contributed immeasurably to shaping our ideals.

The Friendship Collective was a group of nurses who gathered to study the meaning and significance of women's friendships in nursing (1987–1989). Members of this group were: Elizabeth Berrey, Peggy Chinn, Cathy Kane, Christine Madsen, Adrienne Roy, Charlene Eldridge Wheeler, and Elizabeth Mathier Wheeler. Throughout this book, there are many references to the experiences of this group and the individuals in it.

Participants in the Feminism and Nursing class at the State University of New York at Buffalo, Spring, 1982 were particularly influential in our determination to see these ideas in print. Anne Montes (now owner and operator of Emma Bookstore), Adrienne Roy, and Penny Bresnick (whom we first met in that class) have remained close friends and have provided the many forms of love and support that have made this work possible.

The Faculty of Nursing at the University of Technology, Sydney, Kuring-Gai Campus in New South Wales, Australia, participated in an important (for us) workshop that gave us new insights about the use of the process in traditional institutions. The department chair, Judy Lumby, made this workshop possible. In a loving and respectful way, she explored with us some of the most difficult aspects of shifting values in a context where patriarchal ideals reign supreme.

During a visit to Deakin University in Geelong, Victoria, Australia, we were also able to explore more fully some of the philosophic ideas that have informed the approaches we describe here. We extend particular appreciation to Pat Hickson and Cheryle Moss for the insights that they have shared with us where feminist values and traditional philosophy intersect.

In the interim time period between the publication of the second and third editions, we relocated geographically to Denver, Colorado. The students and faculty of the School of Nursing at the University of Colorado have been a particularly important influence on the development of the ideas in this edition. The school's educational, research, and service programs are built on a value of human caring. Unlike many such educational communities, there is explicit commitment to addressing issues openly. Like many such educational communities, there are many issues to address. We appreciate all of the faculty and the students who have worked with us to begin to create new realities within this context.

Prologue

Copper Woman warned Hai Nai Yu that the world would change and times might come when Knowing would not be the same as Doing. And she told her that Trying would always be very important.

Anne Cameron[1]

A few women, old now, and no longer strong. A few elder women who kept alive what the invader tried to destroy. Grandmothers and aunts. Mothers and sisters. Who must be honoured and cherished and protected even at risk of your own life. Who must be respected. At all times respected. Women who know that which we must try to learn again. Women who provide a nucleus on which we must build again. Women who will share with us if we ask them. Women who love us. And seeming candidates, who have been tested and found worthy, and who are learning the old wisdom. Young women who do not always manage to Do that they Know, and so need our love and help.

Anne Cameron[2]

Women's wisdom is ageless and timeless, and passes from generation to generation primarily by oral tradition. Women's wisdom is all too often the hidden foundation of patriarchal scholarship throughout academic, religious, and philosophic literature—without credit to the origins of the ideas. These origins are grounded in women's experiences, female symbolism, and the spiritual roots of the Triple Goddess.[3] One of the most devastating results of this fragmentation and wrongful claiming of ownership of women's wisdom is the use of this wisdom in partial ways.

Women in the feminist tradition have been and are continuing to re-member[4] the wisdom of Doing what we Know, and of Knowing what we Do, moving toward woman-affirming realities. While we may not always manage to Do what we Know, the wisdom survives and is being re-learned with every attempt, with every re-attempt. The Knowing is so deeply buried within us, under layers and layers of patriarchal learning and conditioning, that the Trying is extremely tedious. It is at the same time exciting, affirming, and encouraging. It becomes easier with every lived experience, especially within the context of a community of loving and protective women. As nurses, our communities have been primarily among nurses. We have found that the roots of women's communities emerge from a foundation of all women as healers.[5]

We believe that one of the reasons that the oral tradition has survived and is still practiced so extensively among women is that telling is indeed a simultaneous act of Knowing and Doing that springs comfortably from women's wisdom. Writing is also a form of communication that can be both Knowing and Doing (albeit a bit more of a challenge!).

The written word provides a form that can be more or less enduring in a concrete way, but at the same time becomes static and seemingly frozen in time and space. A major limitation of the written word is that it can be readily destroyed. For centuries, women scholars have recorded women's wisdom into written form, but much of that writing has not survived.[6]

The spoken word, while seeming to disappear once the words are spoken, endures within the heart and mind of the listener and the speaker. Once spoken, it cannot be destroyed unless every person who has heard those words is destroyed. Speaking can also be an interaction, as the speaker and the listener attend to the responses of one another. The act of speaking is an emergence, a creating and a form that gives rise to new acts, new thoughts, and new forms even as the speech occurs. The act of listening—hearing another's words into expression—facilitates a co-creation and allows a fine-tuning of ideas that combines each person's perceptions as words are shared.

This book grew out of our desire to document in writing the women's wisdom that has been passed on to us in the oral tradition and through living examples. We have woven together a wide array of feminist thought that gives form and substance to what we Know and Do. The ideas emerge from depths of experience and knowing within our Selves and from feminist literature (see Notes at the end of the book). In the second edition, we began to draw on our more recent work with the Process, as well as on criticisms and feedback from other women. In this, the third edition, we have continued to incorporate our learning from others, including women in Canada and Australia. We hope the feedback shared by those women has enhanced this edition by providing more global relevance.

In our experience, Doing that which comes from women's Knowing is difficult within the hostile environment of patriarchal systems. We are too familiar with patriarchally structured meetings where we have been out-voted, out-shouted, and unheard. We have eventually dropped out, if not physically, in spirit. No doubt, you have had similar experiences.

Within feminist groups, we have experienced wonderfully different ways of relating, where no one is out-voted, out-shouted, or unheard. Sometimes we have physically dropped out of these groups as our interests or circumstances changed. However, we have always remained in spirit.

We believe that at this point in history, it is critical for women to come together and create woman-affirming interactions and realities. We see small group interactions among women as an ideal place to enact feminist values in a loving and supportive environment.

Language is crucial to creating this environment. For the most part, patriarchal words are what women must use to express our own meanings and wisdom. In the attempt to reflect our own experience, women are creating new meanings and new words. When the listener does not comprehend the meanings, women depend on both actions and speaking to make those meanings clear.

In this book, we use both old words with new (women's) meanings, and new words created to more fully express women's meanings. As a reader, you will not be able to observe our actions that enriched our comprehension, but you will, as you begin to create the process in your own time and space, begin to comprehend and create meanings that emerge from your own wisdom and experience.

To emphasize the importance of women working together to learn and create realities based on feminist values, we use female nouns and pronouns. One issue that we have struggled with is the use of "we," "us," and "our." Sometimes (as in this chapter) these words mean we, as authors, our ideas as authors, and so on. In other sections of the book, these pronouns refer to *all* who share a commitment to the values of Peace and Power. While we have tried to be mindful to be clear and consistent, we (as authors) are relying on you (as readers) to sort it out where we have not been particularly clear!

Just as we learned this process, we have passed this knowledge to other women in words and action—defining, clarifying, and describing as we all participated in the process together. It feels awkward to us to define the process by its parts, but we do not know a better way—in writing—to give a total picture.

This third edition of the *Handbook* includes refinements of language and expression that evolved from our ever-expanding consciousness. It also expands on the ideas in the second edition, and includes several new sections. The first two chapters of the *Handbook* provide the Ideas upon which the Process is built. Chapter 3 describes what it means to make the commitment to feminist values and process. Chapter 4 gives guidelines for forming a group's Principles of Unity. Chapters 5 through 8 provide a description of each component of the Process in action. Chapter 9 provides suggestions for transforming conflict through the process of honoring diversity within the group and developing unity. Chapter 10 gives brief guidelines for periodic transitions, such as changes in group membership. Chapter 11 explores the power of this Process to change existing patriarchal systems, particularly in classrooms, committees, and other groups within existing institutions. There are many adaptations that are needed. Usually, the ideals of *Peace and Power* are realized only partially within these settings. But our experience, and that of many others who have talked or written to us about their use of the process in these settings, confirms that even the slightest inclusion of feminist values in such situations creates an enormous shift toward a different way of interacting.

We have had numerous conversations where women have breastified[7] about their experiences with the Process and the power that comes from trusting in the Process. These groups include administrative team meetings, book discussion groups, hospital ethics committees, child and adult church groups, peace groups, doctoral student study groups, faculty work groups, community service groups, support groups, nursing research groups, and groups writing for publication. We were surprised at times at the wide range of groups that have boldly endorsed the principles and ideals of Peace and Power and have had such wonderful success stories to share.

Finally, the Notes at the end of the book provide the traditional "references" to literature and individual women who we quote, cite, or have influenced our thinking. These notes also provide anecdotal commentary about the text itself, parenthetical ideas related to the text, experiences that inform the text, and literature that provides additional in-depth information about topics in the text. Like the traditions that have emerged in the work of other feminist authors, the notes are a valuable resource of information and, we think, quite readable in their own right.

Throughout, we provide examples from our own experience with the Process. The examples are composites of different experiences and illustrate critical insights. These examples are intended to clarify a simple—but certainly not easy—process.

The re-writing of the third edition occurred during a time when the United States entered into another war. When the war "ended," peace did not exist. This is yet another grim reminder that peace is not merely the absence of war. In our own way, wanting to make a contribution to peace, we talked with many women who were also eager to explore how we can each contribute to creating peace on earth, by beginning within, where we live and work, everyday, in a way that builds on the values of Peace and Power.[8] As we began to more fully act on the ideas that came from these discussions, we came to new realizations about what it means to "Know what I Do, and Do what I Know." We share here some ideas that emerged during this time:

A DOZEN AND ONE IMPORTANT THINGS
YOU CAN DO TO CREATE PEACE ON EARTH

1. Plant and nurture something that grows.
2. Practice the fine art of yielding—in your car, in conversation, and so on.
3. Become active in a group that works on principles of cooperation.
4. Fill your home, work, and commuting environments with visual and auditory images of peace and tranquility.
5. Do at least one thing to simplify your life *and* reduce your consumption of disposable products.
6. Do at least one thing to reduce your consumption of natural resources.
7. Move toward a vegetarian diet.
8. Learn and practice some form of meditation.
9. Learn and practice ways to reduce hostile interactions with others.
10. Exchange gentle forms of touch regularly.
11. Express appreciation to at least one individual or group every day.
12. Help three children learn three things on this list.
13. Pass this list along to someone else.

While writing and revising this book, we have been keenly aware that we cannot directly address the questions or thoughts that might arise as you read, something we would be able to do in a group where we could interact. Since the first edition, we have received many comments, suggestions, insights, and criticisms from women who have used the book. We have integrated these ideas that many have contributed to this work-in-process. We encourage and welcome your criticisms and responses to this new edition.

1

What It's All About: PEACE

If I believe so much must change, I must be willing to change myself.

Frances Moore Lappé, 1990[1]

Can we be like drops of water falling on the stone
Splashing, breaking, dispersing in air
Weaker than the stone by far
But be aware that as time goes by
The rock will wear away
And the water comes again

Meg Christian and Holly Near, 1976[2]

Peace is both the intent and the process from which feminist activism arises. To fully enact *Peace* requires that as individuals we act with conscious awareness as we approach group interactions and Know what it is that we as individuals, acting in concert with others, want to Do. *Peace* is the means and the end, the process and the product. By enacting, we also create.

The acronym that follows defines the idea of *Peace* as intent/process. This acronym builds on an understanding of our feminist concept of what Peace is and what it is not. Each of the components of the acronym reflects a commitment that guides the ways in which individuals can choose to relate to one another within the context of group process. Each letter of the word PEACE represents a concept of the intent/process from which actions arise:

1

Praxis

Empowerment

Awareness

Consensus

Evolvement

PRAXIS

Praxis is thoughtful reflection and action that occur in synchrony, in the direction of transforming the world.[3] Most of us have limited knowledge of praxis, since we exist in a time when "knowing" and "doing" are rarely the same. In Western cultures, we are all familiar with the message "Do as I say, not as I do." When we choose to convey the message that: "I Know what I do, and I Do what I Know," we are living our values. We define praxis as *values made visible through deliberate action*. Thus, praxis used with feminist values becomes an ongoing cycle of constant renewal. As actions are informed by awareness of values, reasons, and ethics, our thinking and our ideas are being shaped and changed by our experiences with those actions.

EMPOWERMENT

Empowerment is growth of personal strength, power, and ability to enact one's own will and love for self in the context of love and respect for others. Empowerment is not self-indulgence, but rather a form of strength that comes from real solidarity with/among those who seek PEACE.[4] Empowerment requires listening inwardly to our own senses as well as listening intently and actively to others, consciously taking in and forming strength.[5] Empowerment is not power over other people, other creatures, or the earth. In fact, empowerment is only possible when individuals express respect and reverence for all other forms of life and ground the energy of the Self as one with the earth.

AWARENESS

Awareness is an active, growing knowledge of Self and others and the world in which we live. For the individual, this necessitates a sharp tuning into the moment. The fundamental method of feminism is consciousness-raising, a vital transformation for women in the context of a society that treats women's knowing and experience as abnormal or nonexistent. With awareness comes a consciousness of "double-speak," where what is defined as "normal" is really abnormal; what is defined as "peace" is really war.[6]

CONSENSUS

Consensus is an active commitment to group solidarity and group integrity. While decision making by consensus is a part of the Process, it is also an internal value that welcomes differences of opinion, and an openness to self-reflection. Perhaps nowhere else are the other elements of PEACE enacted more fully than in bringing our full awareness to preparing for reaching consensus.

A group's commitment to decision making by consensus grows out of mutually defined Principles of Unity where each individual's viewpoint is equally valued when group decisions are made. It means moving away from any action that exerts power over other individuals or groups. Rather, consensus grows from a full integration, a coming to terms, with all perceptions that bear on a particular concern, issue, or decision.[7]

EVOLVEMENT

Evolvement is a commitment to growth, where change and transformation are conscious and deliberate. Evolvement can be likened to the cycles of the moon, where new and old, life and death, and all phases are ultimately one. What remains constant is the cycle itself. As we experience one another within the context of group interaction, we are changed, especially as we engage in Praxis. A group changes as individuals move in and out or become more or less involved, and as purposes or activities change. Growth and transformations are valued and celebrated with each new cycle.[8] Foundational to this valuing is the notion that we are creating our realities as we live them, thus "there can be no mistakes," only opportunities for re-creation.

PEACE IS NOT . . .

- Letting things slide for the sake of friendship.
- Doing whatever is required to keep on good terms.
- Criticizing someone behind her back.
- Being silent at a meeting only to rant and rave afterwards.
- Letting things drift if they don't affect you personally.
- Playing safe in order to avoid confrontation.
- Manipulating someone to avoid open conflict.
- Coercing someone to do what you want.
- Hearing distortions of truth without refuting them.
- Indulging another's behavior when it is destructive.
- Withholding information in order to protect someone else.

HAVING GOOD INTENTIONS IS NOT ENOUGH

Having the intent of *Peace* is critical when you are entering a group interaction. However, intent is not enough. Actions that flow from intent are essential; actions are the critical test of intent. Examine how fully your actions flow with your intent by asking questions such as:

- Do I Know what I Do, and do I Do what I Know? (Praxis)
- Am I expressing my own will in the context of love and respect for others? (Empowerment)

- Am I fully aware of myself and others? (Awareness)
- Do I face conflicts openly and integrate differences in forming solutions? (Consensus)
- Do I value growth and change for myself, others, and the group? (Evolvement)

2

How We Get There from Here: POWER

This transition in our concept of power is radical. It involves seeing power not as a property we own, not as something we exert over others, but as a verb, a process we participate in. This is a huge evolutionary shift.

Joanna Rogers Macy[1]

The challenge for us in developing our personal power is our willingness to recognize that power is within us and in our courageous choice to forgive and release anything that prevents this power from fully manifesting.

Diane Mariechild[2]

We must build a new model of power that is defined as presence: presence of awareness of my own strengths and weaknesses, a deep respect for the SELF of me and therefore a respect for the SELF of others. We must journey toward the individual wholeness of each within the group structure. We must soften and/or relax the barrier between the intellect and the emotions so that the powerful and wonderful material of the unconscious becomes available to the individual and the group. We must be present to self and to others. Power in and of itself is neutral. We must take responsibility for our own actions and choose to know our own intent and the intent of any group before we simply follow a plan of action. Power-over demands that we do things we don't

7

choose to do. Power-of-presence means we choose carefully and understand our intentions.

Grace R. Rowan[3]

Power is the commitment from which feminist activism arises. There are alternatives to the definition and exercise of power as we have learned it in the world at large.[4] While the feminist alternatives are familiar to all of us, we are not accustomed to thinking of them as power because of our experiences and our learning in the traditions of the patriarchal power model. In a sense, the alternative powers should not be called "alternatives" because they are so central and vital to every woman's reality. We call them alternatives only because they are not yet the predominant mode of action in the world at large.

Even though the feminist alternatives may seem idealistic when viewed through cobwebs of patriarchal thinking, they do create dramatic changes when used in the context of a group mutually committed to enacting these powers. It is difficult, but not impossible, to overcome what we have learned to "know" with our heads and to recognize the value of learning what we Know with our heads and hearts.

The feminist alternatives are not opposites, but they do contrast sharply with the patriarchal model. In the column on the left, we list features of patriarchal power and give some familiar examples. In the column on the right, we describe the contrasting feminist alternative with a focus on the values, as well as the process through which they are translated into action.[5]

Patriarchal Power	*Feminist Alternative*
The *Power of Results* emphasizes programs, goals, or policies that achieve the desired results. Achievement of the goals justifies the use of any means: "I don't care how you do it, just get the job done."	The *Power of Process* emphasizes a fresh perspective and freedom from rigid schedules. Goals, programs, and timetables are used as tools, but are less important than the process itself.

Patriarchal Power	*Feminist Alternative*
The *Power of Prescription* imposes change by authority; vested interests prescribe the outcome. The attitude is paternalistic: "Do as I say, I know what is best for you."	The *Power of Letting Go* encourages change emerging out of awareness of collective integrity; leadership inspires a balance between the interests of each individual and the interests of the group; between self-knowledge and cooperation.
The *Power of Division* emphasizes centralization, resulting in the hoarding of knowledge and skills by the privileged few: "What they don't know won't hurt them."	The *Power of the Whole* values the flow of new ideas, images and energy from all, nurturing mutual help networks that are both intimate and expansive. The sharing of knowledge and skills is viewed as healthy and desirable.
The *Power of Force* invests power for or against others and is accomplished by a willingness to impose penalties and negative sanctions. One individual makes decisions on behalf of another individual or group of individuals: "Do it or else."	The *Power of Collectivity* values the personal power of each individual. A group decision where each individual has participated in reaching consensus is viewed as more viable than a decision made by any one individual and stronger than a decision made by a majority.
The *Power of Hierarchy* requires a linear chain of command where layer upon layer of responsibilities are subdivided into separate and discreet areas of responsibility: "I don't make the decisions, I just work here." Or "The buck stops here."	The *Power of Unity* shares the responsibility for decision making and for acting upon those decisions in a lateral network. This process values thoughtful deliberation and emphasizes the integration of variety within the group through the process of transforming conflict.

Patriarchal Power	*Feminist Alternative*
The *Power of Command* requires that leaders are aggressive and followers are passive; leaders are assigned titles, status, and privilege (and higher pay!): "I will tell you what to do." Or "Tell me what to do."	The *Power of Sharing* encourages leadership to shift according to talent, interest, ability, or skill; emphasizes the passing along of knowledge and skills in order that all may develop individual talent.
The *Power of Opposites* polarizes issues. Individual preferences are subsumed by the requirement to make choices "for or against." Language reflects the values of "good versus bad," "right versus wrong": "If you aren't with us, then you are against us."	The *Power of Integration* views situations in context without arbitrary value-laden judgments. In the process of enacting self-volition, the individual integrates the qualities of self-love with love-for-others and acts with respect for each individual's entitlement to self-volition.
The *Power of Use* encourages the exploitation of resources and people as "normal" and acceptable: "If you don't want to work for what we are willing to pay, then quit. There are plenty of people standing in line wanting this job."	The *Power of Nurturing* views life and experience as a resource to be cherished and respected. The earth and all Her creatures are viewed as integral to continued existence on this planet.
The *Power of Accumulation* views material goods, resources, and dollars as "things" to be used in one's own self-interest, as well as items to gain privilege over others: "I worked for it, I bought it, I own it."	The *Power of Distribution* values material resources (including food, land, space, money) as items to use for the benefit of all, to share equitably and according to need. Material goods are valued as a means, not as an end in and of themselves.

Patriarchal Power	*Feminist Alternative*
The *Power of Causality* relies on technology to conquer without regard to the consequences that might be carried over into the future. "Oh, the Pill is causing you to retain fluid? Here, take another pill, this will make you lose fluid."	The *Power of Intuition* senses which actions to take based on the perceived totality of human experience. While technology is considered to be a resource, it is not elected for its own sake or merely because it exists.
The *Power of Expediency* emphasizes the immediate reward or easiest solution. "Oh, radioactive waste? Let's just ship it somewhere else or dump it in the sea."	The *Power of Consciousness* considers long-range outcomes and ethical behaviors. Ethics and morality are derived from feminist values and are the basis for confronting destructive actions and for creating actions that are biophilic.
The *Power of Xenophobia* (the fear of strangers) rewards conformity and adjustment; looking alike and thinking alike are considered as positive assets. "Be a team player. Don't make waves."	The *Power of Diversity* encourages creativity, values alternative views, and encourages flexibility. The expression of dissenting views is expected and all points of view are integrated into decisions.
The *Power of Secrets* relies on the mystification of the process, agents, and the chain of command. The agent who actually has the power rarely implements the decisions or takes direct action, but assigns the dirty work to someone else: "I'm just doing what I was told."	The *Power of Responsibility* focuses on demystification of the processes and insists on naming and/or being the agent; open criticism and self-criticism is encouraged, motivated by love and protection for the individual and the group.

3

Doing It: Making the Commitment

Have you ever . . .

- Been in a meeting where two people argued for most of the time and nothing ever got done?
- Been at a meeting where you never heard what someone was trying to say because she kept getting interrupted?
- Voted against a motion that passed, knowing that your concerns were serious but never heard or addressed?
- Left a meeting thinking that you were the only one who was dissatisfied?
- Left a meeting and then found out in the hall afterwards what was really going on?
- Left a meeting thinking, *"There has got to be a better way?"*

There *is* a better way. The better way is Feminist Process—the concepts of *Peace* and *Power* in action. However, this Process is not a guarantee of totally satisfactory outcomes, nor is it an automatic solution to the dreadful meetings we have all experienced. In fact, the methods we describe, if used in a cookbook manner, will certainly fail.

Creating a better way begins with individuals who consciously choose the values they want to enact *and* take personal responsibility for making it happen. The Process *will* work to create more satisfactory ways of interacting in groups, but its success depends upon each individual taking deliberate responsibility to enact the values of Peace and Power within her own behavior. The problems we experience in traditional groups do not necessarily arise from evil intent, rather they arise from the values we have learned about patriarchal power-over relations. When these values are translated into action, they serve to divide us from one another.

Throughout the remainder of the *Handbook,* we focus on the ideal of creating a new reality through actions based on alternative feminist values. In Chapters 9 and 11, we provide specific suggestions for confronting patriarchal values, and for making a shift toward consciously chosen feminist values. Whether a group is working voluntarily toward full enactment of the ideal, or they are working partially with feminist alternatives as a means to confront patriarchal traditions, the starting point is to own the value or values upon which actions are based.

THE COMMITMENT OF PEACE AND POWER

Moving toward feminist values in a group begins with consciously embracing individual commitment to:

Praxis

Empowerment

Awareness

Consensus

Evolvement

These commitments (described in Chapter 1) represent the values from which feminist ideas of *Power* emerge. Embracing *Peace* internally leads to conscious commitment to feminist values in action and behavior, creating new realities in group interactions. While there are no prescriptions or "recipes" for how an individual is to act or behave in a group, it is possible to describe traits and types of actions that tend to emerge from the commitment to Peace and Power. Having an idea about what each individual can do to make the new reality happen, helps each person begin to enact her own choices. In this chapter, we focus on the internal work of the individual in relation to the group process, and the individual actions and behaviors that arise from the commitment to do this work. The following examples are not all inclusive. We are confident that you will be able to add to the list in important ways.

A commitment to the *Power of Process* means:

- Giving yourself and everyone else in the group the time to attend to a concern or issue that exists for any individual.
- Letting decisions emerge gradually, realizing that very few decisions are urgent.
- Inviting everyone in the group to express their ideas or concerns during the discussion.

A commitment to the *Power of Letting Go* means:

- Moving away from your own vested interests in order for others in the group to express their interests fully.
- Supporting others who are new, or learning something new, in their work of taking on something you are already skilled at doing.
- Expressing your misgivings or concerns about a situation in the group, but letting the sense of the group prevail when the group needs to move on to something else.

A commitment to the *Power of the Whole* means:

- Placing your own individual needs and interests within the context of the group.
- Encouraging working together to equalize power within the group and create empowerment for all.

A commitment to the *Power of Collectivity* means:

- Taking into account the interests of every member of the group, including those who are not present.
- Making sure that every concern has been addressed and fully integrated into every discussion and decision.

A commitment to the *Power of Unity* means:

• Addressing conflict openly, and in so doing working actively to strengthen the integrity of the group.

• Celebrating values and joys that are shared in common.

• Keeping the group's Principles of Unity in conscious awareness as a basis for moving forward.

A commitment to the *Power of Sharing* means:

• Taking responsibility for leadership and tasks, including things you enjoy doing and can do well, as well as things you would rather not do but that need to be done.

• Encouraging others to join in passing skills and tasks along, by assuming tasks from others.

A commitment to the *Power of Integration* means:

• Listening actively and deliberately to every concern or idea that others bring to the group, and taking active steps to understand and act on others' points of view.

• Taking actions that encourage bringing things together, rather than polarizing them into opposing points of view.

A commitment to the *Power of Nurturing* means:

• Treating one another in ways that convey love and respect.

• Acknowledging that each individual's experience has uniquely qualified her to be where she is at the present.

• Affirming and rejoicing in the knowledge that each woman in the group has her own power to use in any way she may choose.

A commitment to the *Power of Distribution* means:

• Taking actions to overcome imbalances in personal material resources among group members.

• Using resources that are available to the group as a means, not an end.

• Making all resources that are available to the group equally available to all in the interest of the development of the group and each individual.

A commitment to the *Power of Intuition* means:

- Taking the time to think, feel, and experience the fullness of a situation.
- Taking actions that seem risky when your gut tells you to go ahead.

A commitment to the *Power of Consciousness* means:

- Talking about why you are doing what you are doing.
- Exploring with others awareness of feelings, situations, responses, and meanings in your experiences.

A commitment to the *Power of Diversity* means:

- Stopping to carefully consider another point of view when your immediate response is to reject it.
- Taking deliberate actions to keep yourself and the group open to creating accessibility for others who are different or new.

A commitment to the *Power of Responsibility* means:

- Keeping everyone in the group fully informed about the group tasks you are doing and about anything in your personal life that might affect the group as a whole.
- Acting to make sure that nothing is mystified, that everything that concerns the group is equally accessible to every member.
- Actively Checking In and Closing in a spirit of contributing to the growth and development of the group.

4

What We Are All About:
Principles of Unity

*. . . Imagine how it feels to always belong—belong in a di-
versified community, for it is the diversity in nature that gives
the web of life its strength and cohesion. Imagine a time where
everyone welcomes diversity in people because they know that
is what gives community its richness, its strength, its cohesion.
Imagine being able to relax into our connectedness—into a
web of mutually supportive relations with each other and
with nature. . . .*

*. . . Imagine a world where there was collective support in
the overcoming of individual limitations, where mistakes
weren't hidden but welcomed as opportunities to learn, where
there was no reason to withhold information, where honesty
was a given. Imagine a world where what is valued most is not
power but nurturance, where the aim has changed from being
in control to caring and being cared for, where the expression
of love is commonplace.*

*. . . The very fact that you can imagine these things makes
them real, makes them possible.*

Margo Adair[1]

Principles of Unity provide a bridge between that which brings us
together as a cohesive group, and that which distinguishes each of
us as individuals. The Principles of Unity provide a grounding from
which the group can focus their energies, the ideals toward which
the group builds, a guide around which to integrate all individual

19

perspectives in forming decisions, a basis for giving one another growthful criticism, and a foundation for transforming diversity into group strength.

Principles of Unity are statements of mutually shared beliefs and agreements that are formed early in the group's experience together. Although it is important to write them down, they are not sealed in stone. They are deliberately and thoughtfully revised and changed as the experience of the group emerges and the needs of the group change.

The Principles are the basis for each part of the group's ongoing process. They also provide an introduction and orientation to individuals who are considering becoming a part of the group. New members may contribute valuable perspectives that can lead to shifts and changes in the Principles, but the Principles form a grounding for stability within the group as membership changes.

The written document that contains the Principles of Unity is kept before the group; each member has a copy and works with it constantly. The document is particularly important as a source for forming constructive criticism (see Chapter 8), and when the group is addressing conflict (see Chapter 9). When each member's copy is almost not readable from the penciled-in changes that emerge over time, it is time to consider having them retyped!

BUILDING PRINCIPLES OF UNITY

Feminist Process is based on a balance between unity within the group and diversity among individuals. Individuals enter a group with differences in style, personality, beliefs, and backgrounds, as well as with some common purpose or motive. In a group committed to feminist process, differences ultimately strengthen the integrity of the group, because the group members value and acknowledge their differences openly and work toward reaching mutual understandings of these differences.

Building Principles of Unity begins with each woman sharing her own ideas about the group, why she is interested in being part of the group, and what she expects from the group. Each perspective is expressed as fully as possible. Then the group begins to identify those ideas around which the group members are clearly unified, and those ideas that represent diversity from which to build common understandings.

Ideally, Principles of Unity are formed in the first few gatherings of a new group. For an existing group that chooses to begin using Feminist Process, the decision to shift to this way of working together is the first step in forming Principles of Unity, and that decision becomes one of the Principles.

In our experience, the time invested to form new Principles of Unity or to re-examine existing Principles of Unity is some of the most valuable time spent in group work. Usually a task-oriented group that will meet regularly for a year or more requires two or three half-day gatherings to form a beginning sct of Principles of Unity, and regular times set aside thereafter to re-evaluate those principles.

There are at least seven components that a group needs to consider in forming Principles of Unity.[2] Each component becomes a section of the written document, but the specific Principles will vary according to the needs and purposes of each group.

Who Are We?

The name of a group implies a great deal about the group. Once a name is selected, the words used in the name may need specific definition. For example, the word "radical" in a group's name might be defined as "fundamental; going to the root."

The group may also need to make an explicit agreement about who the individuals within the group are or will be in the future. For example, a group that is formed to create and maintain a women's center in the community may deliberately seek participation from a broad base of women in the community, including women of color, women of all sexual preferences, women of differing economic classes, and so forth. A support group for lesbians will likely define their group identity as lesbian; a group that is working on the rights of lesbian mothers may actively seek the participation of nonlesbians as well as lesbians who are not mothers.

An important dimension of defining membership is getting clear on how open the group is to integrating new members, when and how this will happen. A group that is formed to accomplish a specific, detailed, and long-term task may need to initially limit membership to a few members who are able and willing to remain dedicated to the accomplishment of the task. While many groups will choose not to be "closed" groups in relation to membership, there may be periods of time where stability in the membership of the group is needed. Making a specific agreement about how long group membership will remain stable is helpful in preventing misunderstandings within the group, as well as in communicating with others who are not group members.

What Are Our Purposes?

Defining who the group is provides a basis for identifying the group's purposes. A women's center group may have the immediate purpose of finding a space, but then the group members need to identify the purposes for which that space will exist and how it will be used. If one purpose is to provide shelter for battered women, there are additional things to be defined in relation to this purpose, such as if the group will offer counseling, economic, legal, or educational services as well.

The group's purposes need to be considered in terms of what is realistic for the initial group. The members of a battered women's support group may want to see the group offer a full range of services to women and their children. However, the resources of the group may be such that the initial purpose needs to be limited to fund-raising and educational work. Being clear at the outset about the limits of the purpose can help the group to use their resources and energies in productive ways, rather than in working at cross-purposes.

In each of the following sections, examples of Principles of Unity are provided from our experience with the Friendship Collective, whose purpose was to study the experience of female friendship among nurses.[3]

What Beliefs and Values Do We Share Around Our Purpose?

Whatever the group defines as its purpose will direct the group toward exploring various values and beliefs related to that purpose.

Certain values are fundamental to a feminist perspective; stating these values is important to help each member of the group grow in her understanding of the meaning of these values. Having the beliefs and values stated provides a way for the group to examine how the shifts represented in feminist values create changes in how we act and how we relate to one another.

The beliefs and values that formed Principles of Unity for the Friendship Collective are:

- We believe that friendships among women are fundamental to female survival and growth.
- We believe that women's friendships that are based on feminist praxis are critical for feminist existence and culture.
- We value all forms of friendship between women.
- We value our own friendships among one another and are committed to living our friendship with deliberate awareness, examining and creating our experience as we go.

What Individual Circumstances or Personal Values Do We Need to Consider as We Work Together?

Having a space where every woman feels safe to speak, to act, and to Be is central to the concept of Feminist Process. This space is essential for the constructive interactions that are central to woman-affirming realities. Given the realities of a male-dominated society, most women's groups must confront the personal issue of male presence, physically and psychologically. The group needs to take the time to explore the range of values of each member, what it means for us as women to be fully present to our own experiences and what barriers prevent us from focusing our energies on our own experiences.

The range of personal values that need to be considered depends on the individuals who are in the group. Differing circumstances of women's lives create varying expectations and commitments. Women who are single parents or who care for older adults may need careful limits on time and other personal resources. Women who need personal support from the group because of crises or difficult personal circumstances may want the group to have more flexibility in relation to time spent together. A woman in a wheelchair not only needs space that is accessible to her, but she also needs the group's awareness of her particular fears and challenges. A woman who suffers from fat oppression may not need specific physical arrangements, but needs the group's awareness of the discriminations she experiences and how these can be overcome within this group. Any woman who is a "minority" within a group, whether on the basis of race, age, ethnicity, sexuality, social class, education, or any other basis, needs recognition and valuing of these differences. Once the group has openly explored the range of personal circumstances of each woman's life, then the group can agree upon a common set of expectations that everyone values.

Examples of Principles of Unity formed by the Friendship Collective that grew out of personal circumstances and individual values are:

- We will not intentionally take any action individually or collectively that exploits any individual within the group or any other women.

- We will keep at a minimum any financial expenses needed from any individual in relation to our work and will openly negotiate these demands as they occur.

- We will be conscious of helping one another maintain a balance between the demands of our group work and our personal lives.

- We will maintain careful time limits for our gatherings that are mutually agreed upon by each member of the group at each gathering.

What Do We Expect of Every Member?

Time, energy, and commitment expectations can take many different forms. For example, group members might be expected to attend a monthly meeting and contribute to the work of a task group that meets about three hours each week. For another group, members might be expected to attend a yearly meeting and work on one project of their choosing during the year. Large groups that do not actually meet, but rather join in a network to promote communication might expect that every member contribute financially to the network, with the work of specific tasks done by smaller groups as they volunteer to assume those responsibilities.

Bringing to conscious awareness ways in which each member is expected to interact within the group is central in forming Principles of Unity. We are accustomed to entering groups with an unspoken ideal that everyone will be "open and honest." In reality, we know that in many groups we find hidden agendas and manipulative behavior. In fact, we know better than to expect immediate openness and honesty; these take time to develop as each person earns the trust that makes openness and honesty possible. Any form of feminist process requires that common expectations for interaction are made explicit, and that they move beyond unrealistic expectations and damaging types of group interactions, especially those that creep in unaware.

Examples of Principles of Unity that grew out of the Friendship Collective's expectations for interactions are:

- We will meet once a week until the initial stage of the project is planned, and at regular intervals thereafter we will renegotiate the frequency of our meetings.

- We will take time to relax and play together.

- We are committed to using feminist process, including making decisions through consensus and learning to provide constructive, growthful criticism for one another.

- We will address conflicts, feelings, and issues between us openly as soon as they reach our awareness, with the understanding that early awareness may not be perfect but deserves expression.

- We will share skills, leadership, and responsibility within the group according to ability and willingness, and will work to nurture these abilities in each of us so that they are shared as equally as possible.

- We welcome any individual assuming specific tasks that need to be done that grow out of our mutually agreed direction, and support her initiative in doing so. We expect that each of us will keep every other member of the group fully informed as to the progress of her activities related to the group's work.

What Message Do We Wish to Convey to the World Outside Our Group?

Every group conveys a message to the rest of the world about who they are and what they are all about. Sometimes the message is accurate to the intents of the group, other times it is not. In a feminist group, the message is formed with careful and deliberate intent, and the group constantly examines the ways in which that message is being conveyed. The message that is sought is always consistent with what the group believes and values, but there are still choices to be made in relation to that message.

For example, a group that exists to develop services for battered women may decide to form a message that emphasizes women as physically strong, powerful, and resourceful. Another component of that message might be that women help other women, providing support and assistance in a wide variety of ways. The ways in which members of the group interact in public will be informed by these two messages as central considerations. These messages would grow out of the beliefs the group has about women in general, as well as beliefs about women who are battered.

Examples of Principles of Unity that the Friendship Collective formed in relation to our message are:

- We will work to form a message that is consistent with what we believe about female friendship and about feminist praxis.
- All public presentations will reflect our cooperative, feminist style of working, and will reflect our commitment to sharing of skills, leadership, and responsibility.
- We will carefully and constructively criticize each public presentation or written document to examine the message we think we actually conveyed, and to re-form our own commitments and our presentation style as needed to more closely convey the message that we intend.

How Will We Protect the Integrity of Our Group?

Groups that are engaged in activist work or that begin to create a new reality for women ultimately encounter outside demands for their time and attention. These demands may place unrealistic burdens on the group, and they may not always be consistent with the direction that the group wishes to take. Conscious awareness and anticipation of these possibilities helps a group to develop agreements that can guide responses to outside demands.

Examples of Principles of Unity formed by the Friendship Collective to protect group integrity are:

- All requests of our group will be discussed in a gathering with all of us present, and all decisions made regarding outside demands will be made by consensus of the group.

- Decisions about outside requests will be informed by a primary concern for the protection of each of us individually, our primary commitment to the work of our group, and our readiness to respond to the request.

- We will maintain our commitment to feminist praxis and to feminist methods in our work, and will carefully examine all situations that might result in an erosion of this commitment.

- We will seek external funding for our work, but will examine the demands placed on us in relation to accepting funding to assure that whatever demands these are, they do not compromise our primary principles.

5

Getting Things Going: Everybody Does It

Feminist Process is an alternative to traditional power structures within groups. Once a group decides to use Feminist Process, each woman must determine her own willingness to work in a disciplined and collective style, her willingness to value and learn from differences among individuals within the group, her commitment to struggle with conflicts openly, her commitment to take ownership for her own behavior, and her reasons and motives for becoming a part of the group.

Each phase of Feminist Process is enacted by individuals who engage in the group with the *intent* of *Peace* and the *commitment* to feminist *Power*. Each phase of the process used for each gathering grows out of a group's Principles of Unity—principles that each individual helps to form or re-form as the group grows.

Groups sit in a circle so that everyone has eye contact.[1] Usually one individual, the Convener, comes to the gathering with an agenda that provides structure for the gathering. This responsibility rotates among group members every gathering. The Process for each gathering has several distinct components that encourage each individual to put Feminist values into practice.

The Convener opens the gathering by beginning Check-In (explained later in this chapter), when each woman declares herself fully Present—in mind, body, and spirit.[2] Check-In is a time for each individual to focus her awareness on the purposes of the gathering, to share with the group any circumstances that might influence her participation in the process, and to bring her individual perspective for this gathering before the group.

Following Check-In, the Convener draws attention to the agenda and begins the process of Rotating Chair (see Chapter 6). Rotating Chair is a mutually shared responsibility for facilitating group interactions. The "chair" refers to whoever is speaking. The primary purpose of Rotating Chair is to promote every woman's viewpoint being heard, with *each* woman's input being valued and necessary.

Group decisions are reached by Consensus (see Chapter 7). Consensus focuses on reaching a conclusion that takes into account all viewpoints and one that is consistent with the group's Principles of Unity. In contrast to compromise, which is a decision that focuses on what each individual gives up, consensus is a process that focuses on what each individual and the group as a whole *gains* by the nature of the decision that is reached. Central to the concept of Feminist Process is the idea that a group decision reached by consensus is more viable than one achieved by a majority vote or by any one individual.

The final component of Feminist Process is Closing, a process of ending a gathering or discussion, and beginning movement toward the next stage of the group's process (see Chapter 8). During Closing, each woman shares her *appreciation* for something that has happened during the process of the gathering, her *criticism* leading toward growth and change, and an *affirmation* that expresses her own personal commitment for moving into the future.

THE CONVENER

The one individual who comes to a gathering with a specifically defined role is the Convener. A different individual volunteers to convene each gathering so that the task rotates and each person develops leadership skills.

The Convener's primary responsibilities are to prepare the agenda for the gathering, to begin Check-In, and in some types of gatherings, present a SOPHIA (described later in this chapter).

During the gathering, the Convener assumes a leadership role, facilitating attention to the mutually agreed upon agenda. The Convener actively listens to the discussion and calls for shifts in the process as facilitator. For example, when the Convener notices that some women have not had an opportunity to speak, she might request a Circling process (see Chapter 6). Or, when she senses that all viewpoints have been heard, she begins the process of decision making by consensus (see Chapter 7).

The agenda can be written on a chalkboard or large sheet of paper (shelf liner or freezer wrap will do!) and posted before the time the gathering is scheduled to begin. The Convener also identifies announcements or items that need to be mentioned without discussion and presents these just after Check-In.

Other members of the group can assume these leadership roles at any time, but the Convener remains particularly attentive to group movement. This does not mean that the Convener behaves like the traditional "Chairman of the Bored"—calling time limits, reminding people to use Rotating Chair, or calling on people to speak. Every individual present is equally responsible for being fully present and willing to speak during the gathering. Once the discussion begins; the Convener is free to participate in the discussion using the process of Rotating Chair (see Chapter 6), just as any other member of the group.

The Convener's unique responsibility is to make conscious choices to provide leadership and to come to the gathering prepared to do so. Providing leadership that is focused on group process means:

- Letting the group know when agreed-on time limits are near.

- Remaining conscious of requests made by individuals for shifts in the agenda, tasks, process shifts, and so on.

- Helping the group to be aware of alternative possibilities throughout the discussion, such as minority viewpoints that have not received full attention, hearing from people who have not spoken to an issue, or choices that have not been considered by the group.

- Suggesting group processes that can move the group along in the process, such as calling for "Circling" or "Sparking."

- Remaining attentive to possibilities for developing consensus, and providing leadership for the group to do so.
- Shifting the focus of the discussion to Closing so that the group has the time they agreed upon for this part of the process.

The following guidelines are for Conveners to use in thinking about and planning for gatherings:

Review the Notes from the Last Gathering:

- Are there items from other gatherings that need to be addressed or items that the group decided to carry over to the next gathering for discussion?
- Are there any new resources needed to enhance the discussions of the items brought forward from the last gathering?
- Has anything happened that will effect the decisions made at the last gathering?

Review Group Process:

- What individual concerns or needs have been expressed that should be considered in planning for this gathering?
- What group issues have women identified that need to be considered in planning for this gathering?
- What group strengths have been identified that need to be sustained and supported during this gathering?

Plan the Agenda:

- What announcements need to be shared?
- Are there special time considerations or other individual needs to be taken into account?
- What new items need to be introduced?
- What specific tasks or responsibilities need to be done before the gathering?

SOPHIA

In groups where discussion is a primary focus, a SOPHIA can be prepared by the Convener in advance of the gathering, and presented after Check-In and after the group has reviewed the agenda. A SOPHIA is a 5- to 10-minute verbal essay that comes from the speaker's own inner wisdom. *Sophia* is the Greek word for wisdom; she was wisdom in ancient western theologies.[3] In the context of discussion groups, we define a SOPHIA as:

S*peak* **O***ut,* **P***lay* **H***avoc,* **I***magine* **A***lternatives*

A SOPHIA is intended to focus the group's attention on the topic of discussion. If the group has shared readings in advance of the discussion, the SOPHIA draws on those readings, but brings the perspective of the speaker to interpret the meaning of the readings for the individual and the group. An important purpose of the SOPHIA is to raise questions for all to consider. The questions are also called "subjectives" (not the traditional "objectives"). Subjectives are critical questions that arise from varying perspectives on the issue under consideration. There are no answers to subjectives, rather, there are many possible responses, all of which will be respectfully considered in the discussion. The SOPHIA, and the subjectives that it contains, offer to the group a wide array of possibilities.

A SOPHIA is particularly useful in a classroom setting, a book discussion group, or a group that is in a muddle about Principles of Unity. You no doubt will find other instances where a SOPHIA is appropriate to open a discussion.

CHECKING-IN

Check-In is:

- Saying what you are prepared to contribute to the group interaction and what you hope for the group during the gathering.

- Sharing circumstances or events that are likely to influence your participation during the discussions.

- Reflecting briefly on what you integrated or gained from the last gathering.

- Actively expressing your commitment to be fully Present for the group during this time together.

- Committing yourself to creating a safe space, arising from your love and respect for each individual and the group.

Check-In is time for the group to hear every individual speak. Check-In usually opens the gathering to assure that concerns of everyone present are fully integrated into the discussion. While Check-In need not consume a great deal of time, enough time needs to be provided so that each individual speaks. Check-In is initiated by the Convener and is an indication to all that the gathering has begun.

Check-In is a brief statement by each individual that centers the attention of the group on the shared purpose for being together. Each woman shares her own specific expectations for the gathering, so that this can be integrated by everyone present. Once this is done, there are no hidden agendas.

For new groups, each person may give her name, something about herself, and her reason for being present. For those joining an established group, Check-In can feel intimidating. A lifetime of patriarchal process creates doubts about how safe any space really is. Until a woman feels comfortable within a group, she may only wish to share who she is and her purpose for being present.

One purpose for "checking-in" is to address your own ability or limits in participating during the gathering. If you are not sure how fully present you are able to be, you might say "I am distracted tonight, but I want to hear the discussion and participate as much as possible." You may choose to provide some details that will facilitate the group's understanding. It is important to say something about what you hope for by being present. Knowing the circumstances that are influencing your ability to attend to the work of the group, and what you are working for on behalf of the group, the group can respond in a supportive and caring way.

There are many other things that may be shared during Check-In. Suppose that during Closing at the end of the last gathering, comments were shared about Sally's constructive way of responding to a situation. Sue reflected on the constructive approach that Sally used and practiced the approach at home. During Check-In, Sue relates what happened and shares with the group that if the situation had not been examined during Closing she would not have been able to change what she had been doing. It is important for the group that Sue share this experience of her own growth, in order for the group to appreciate the far-reaching influences of their collective actions.

Responding to Check-In

Check-In does not occur in a vacuum. The group briefly focuses energy, time, and attention to what each individual has expressed. Some Check-Ins may require more energy and time than others; some may require no response. When women have exciting good news, the group may wish to express their shared joy. When a woman is preoccupied with some circumstance that may interfere with her participation, the group may inquire "How can we best respond right now" to help clarify what kind of response might be best for the individual and the group. If a woman shares a dramatic and important event—such as the death of a friend—the group may wish to suspend the agenda entirely or alter the agenda in some way.

CHECK-OUT

We use the notion of Check-Out in two ways. First, if a woman is not able to participate in the gathering in an active way, she should Check-Out entirely, either from this gathering or from the group altogether. Sleeping or reading a book during a gathering does not constitute participation!

While every individual's Check-In differs in extent and detail, it is vital for each woman to share something about her intent for each gathering. Silence during Check-In leaves others wondering what you are thinking and leaves room for doubts about your intents. Silence during Check-In interferes with creating a safe space. If you really can't participate with a spirit of owning your part of responsibility for the group process then it is time to Check-Out of the group.

Another kind of Check-Out occurs when a woman is present and committed to the group but has specific limits on her time and energy for a particular gathering. If you come to a gathering and have to leave at some point before Closing, then explain your situation during Check-In and give the time frame you are committed to. As the time nears, request the chair and share any closing comments. Give the group time to attend to your concerns, unfinished business, or to make plans for finishing something you might be involved with.

For example, a gathering has been scheduled to end at 10:00 PM. Neva wishes to leave the meeting at 9:00 PM because she is taking an exam the next morning and needs to get a good night of rest. Neva has been involved in planning for a concert that the group is sponsoring and wants to be present for that discussion. She shares her circumstance with the group and requests that the discussion about the concert be placed earlier than planned on the agenda so that she can be present for it. The group agrees to this priority and the gathering proceeds. As 9:00 PM draws near, Neva requests the chair and shares with the group that she is concerned that there are still some loose ends related to the concert. The group shifts attention to Neva's comments, wraps up the loose ends, and wishes her the best on her exam.

6

Turning It Over: Rotating Chair

Rotating Chair is truly "turning it over." Using Rotating Chair turns upside-down the long-accepted custom of hierarchical structures—a linear chain of command where a single individual or an elite group assumes leadership and control. Rotating Chair turns over to each member of the group the rights and responsibilities for leadership, tasks, and decisions.

The process of Rotating Chair may initially seem awkward, cumbersome, inefficient, and a nuisance. We are certain that it is especially tedious to attempt to learn this process by reading. (As we were writing, we increasingly appreciated the oral tradition!) Once you experience the entire process in the context of a group with mutual intent and commitment to feminist values, concerns and reservations about the process gradually disappear. In fact, it becomes excruciating to try to endure the old ways when dealing with the world at large.

ROTATING CHAIR

Rotating Chair is a mutually shared responsibility for group participation and interaction. Whoever is speaking is the Chair. Following Check-In, the Convener focuses on any announcements. The group then reviews the agenda and identifies any items that need to be included that are not on the agenda, or re-orders the agenda

37

based on things shared during Check-In. If anyone has a brief item that simply consists of information sharing, this is a good time to do so. The group may set time limits and priorities on the agenda items.

In discussion groups, the Convener then shares her SOPHIA. The questions shared at the end of a SOPHIA often spark discussion. In task-oriented groups, the Convener focuses the group's attention on the first item of business. Then the Chair rotates to whoever wishes to speak and discussion begins. The Chair continues to rotate to members of the group who wish to speak.

Once the discussion begins, a group member expresses her desire to speak by raising her hand. The woman who is speaking is responsible for passing the Chair to the next individual who raises her hand. The Chair is passed by calling the name of the group member you are recognizing to speak next. If more than one person indicates a desire to speak, preference is given to the person who has not spoken or who has not spoken recently.

Passing the Chair by calling of names is an important tool for a large group to help everyone learn everyone's name. In any size group, it is a symbolic gesture that signifies honoring each individual's identity, and respecting the Presence of each woman. Calling the next speaker's name is also a clear signal that you have finished speaking, and that you are indeed passing the Chair along.

A speaker is not obligated to relinquish the Chair to someone else until she has completed the ideas and thoughts she wishes to share. At the same time, each speaker has the responsibility to make way for all who are present to speak to each issue. Each speaker avoids making long, repetitive, or unrelated comments that prevent access to the Chair for other women.

During the discussion, make notes of your thoughts and allow the person speaking to complete her thoughts before you indicate your desire to speak. In this way, you can attend more fully to the speaker's ideas and allow her the time and space to fully express her concerns. Frantically waving your hand in eagerness to share your thought is just as distracting and disrespectful as verbally interrupting.

At first, raising your hand can make you feel as if you have gone back to kindergarten. You may initially find hand-raising awkward and intimidating. The benefits, however, soon become apparent. Each woman speaking can be confident that she will be heard, that she may complete her thoughts without interruption and that she will not be intimidated by someone with a louder voice. Each woman desiring to speak is assured that she will have the opportunity to do so. A woman with a soft voice knows that she doesn't have to shout to get attention. A woman who is unaccustomed to speaking in a group is assured of having a space and the time to practice those skills. A woman who speaks slowly, or who pauses to gather her thoughts, is assured that nobody is going to jump in and grab the attention of the group before she completes what she wants to say.

PASSING IT ALONG: NOTES, MINUTES, AND ARCHIVES

Everyone who participates in a gathering takes her own notes. These notes facilitate the process of Rotating Chair, but they are not a record of the meeting and are not generally shared with the group. They are used as a personal tool to remain in touch with thoughts you have while others are speaking. Your own notes make it possible for you to hold on to an idea that you want to share, without interrupting someone else who is speaking. They form a personal journal of your experiences. They can also serve as a personal reminder of what it is you have agreed to do! These notes are a valuable resource during Closing, making possible your recall of specific process issues you want to speak to.

For a task-oriented group, at least one individual assumes the responsibility for recording the proceedings of the gathering in the form of Minutes. For gatherings that last longer than about an hour at a stretch, it is helpful to share this task among different individuals in the group. Other kinds of groups may or may not decide to have group minutes.

There are several reasons for keeping Minutes:

1. To provide a permanent record for the group's archives;
2. To communicate information to those women who are not present at the gathering, so they can be informed of what happened;

3. To provide a reference for the Convener of the next gathering; and

4. To help those with short memories figure out what they are supposed to do next!

Some groups keep detailed records of all ideas and comments, including who spoke and a summary of what she said. Other groups keep simple records of who was present at the gathering, the decisions made, and the major factors that contributed to each decision. The group's needs may vary from one gathering to the next.

ACTIVE LISTENING

Active listening is a vital part of the process of Rotating Chair. This requires deliberate awareness of how you perceive what other women say. Whenever you are not sure if your perception is accurate, request the Chair and ask for clarification. It is helpful to paraphrase in your own words what you understood, so that the woman who was speaking does not have to wonder what you thought she said. Once you have paraphrased what you heard, any misunderstanding can be identified and clarified either by the woman who spoke initially or by others.

THE TYRANNIES OF SILENCE AND REPETITION

It is difficult for the group to get a sense of group consensus if women consistently do not speak to issues. Silence, when your viewpoint has not been expressed, deprives the group of the benefit of a viewpoint that might not otherwise be taken into account. Remember, this process does not function on the notions of "majority" and "minority." Even if you are the only one who holds an opinion, this must be taken into account in decision making. *Every* viewpoint is taken into account regardless of how many or how few hold that viewpoint.

At the same time, it is not necessary for every individual to address every issue. If your viewpoint has already been expressed, you need not repeat what has already been said, although it is often important that you indicate to the group that you agree with what someone else has already said. If you agree but have a different thought or concern to add, you need to speak to have your additional thought considered in the discussion.

DIALOGUE

When only two people are present, dialogue is highly desirable. In a group larger than two, dialogue becomes destructive to group process and usually models power-over tactics of traditional meetings. Dialogue in a group promotes argument and debate between individuals and prevents other viewpoints from being heard. The process of Rotating Chair honors each woman's input as valuable and necessary.

When two women are in energetic opposition to one another's positions, it is time to have other voices heard. Conflict can be growthful and desirable (see Chapter 9), but dialogue between two individuals in conflict leads to getting caught up in the conflict itself. As other women speak, the group is able to define what the issue really is. At the same time, the two women who are in conflict have an opportunity to reflect on their own positions, hear the thoughts and feelings of other group members, and to decide if their thoughts and feelings are helping or hindering group process.

There are situations when one or two individuals have specific information about a certain issue. Directing a question to an individual and engaging in information exchange is not the same as dialogue. Information exchange is simply that—information exchange. However, when a group consistently defers to one or two individuals as the "knowledgeable ones," it is a signal that sharing of information and skills is not happening. The group needs to give attention to providing the opportunity for everyone to share her point of view or information.

VARIATIONS

There are no rules in Rotating Chair; however, there are behaviors we have found to be effective in expressing the feminist values and intents of Peace and Power. In addition to the central methods of passing along the chair in Rotating Chair, variations can be used to bring flexibility to the process.

Variations are often needed when the group is small (fewer than six), or large (more than 35). Small groups tend to be less formal, and often rely on "dinner table" styles of discussion. When this happens, everyone gets to speak, but the discussion may wander. In large groups, some people do not have the opportunity to speak, and shy people may find it very difficult to speak.

The following are variations that we have found helpful in a number of circumstances. You will surely find other variations as well!

Sparking

When an issue or a topic generates a great deal of excitement in the group, the discussion often moves naturally into a style that reflects the high energy of excitement. Many individuals begin to speak, sometimes at once, often tossing words and ideas into the air like a fountain.

This type of discussion is *Sparking.* When it begins to happen naturally, it should be left alone as long as the discussion is providing the group with new ideas and energy to move forward. Once some individuals begin to lose interest, or the ideas are beginning to be repetitive, it is time for the Convener or another group member to assume leadership, asking the group to cease Sparking and return to the more focused style of Rotating Chair.

Sometimes an individual brings an idea or topic to the group that needs "Sparking." She can ask the group to enter this style of discussion for a specific period of time, or plan to include Sparking around the idea at a future gathering.

Sparking is a valuable process for creating ideas and energy, but it does not work well to help everyone participate equally, or to be heard. When it is used, it needs to be used with deliberate intent, with everyone in the group aware that this is what is going on. When it is time to cease, Circling may be used as a transition back to Rotating Chair.

Circling

Circling is a time when open discussion and rotation of the chair is suspended, and *everyone* in the group takes a turn around the circle to speak to an issue. Although it is usually the Convener, any group member who perceives that the group needs to focus and clarify may request the group to "Circle." Whoever calls for a Circle then shares her perception of what the focus of the Circle needs to be.

Everyone speaks very briefly, with her comments limited to the focus for which Circling has been requested. This provides for the group a connection with each woman's point of view at that point in time. It also provides a few moments for each individual to get clearer in her own thinking. Even if some women have nothing specific to contribute at this time, it is important that everyone at least share their perceptions with the group.

When the discussion seems to be nearing time for consensus but this is not yet clear, someone can request a circle to simply find out if women feel ready to form consensus on the issue. At the end of Sparking, Circling can be a time for everyone to share which of the ideas expressed "sparked" the most for her.

Circling is especially helpful when tensions are running high, with two or three women at the center of the struggle. Circling can be used to interrupt the dialogue that often begins during times of tension. Circling gives every individual in the group the responsibility and the opportunity to speak, to share her insights at the moment, or to express feelings that may not already be apparent. Circling provides the opportunity for women at the center of the struggle to listen attentively to the perspectives that others have to offer, and time to do some inner work with respect to the struggle.

Circling can be used to begin the process of bringing closure to an issue, with everyone sharing her thinking on the issue before ending the discussion and moving to another agenda item, to Consensus, or to Closing.

Timing-Call

Despite our best intentions, individuals sometimes do get carried away in speaking to an issue. If a group is having difficulty with extended "mini-speeches" that interfere with everyone having the opportunity to speak, they can agree to use a Timing-Call signal— a simple "T" formed with the hands—to help the speaker remember to bring her comments to a close so that others can speak.

A conscious decision to use a Timing Call avoids slipping into unconscious patterns of interacting. A common unconscious habit that is used to try to interrupt long-winded speakers is hand-waving to ask for the Chair while the speaker is still speaking. Not only is hand-waving disrespectful of the speaker, it is disruptive to the process and to the group. Hand-waving is a competitive gesture on the part of one who also wants to speak.

When a group consciously recognizes that long-winded speeches are interfering with their process, then a consciously chosen signal is a respectful way to begin to shift the patterns of interaction on the part of individuals. The Timing Call is not a signal requesting the chair; it is simply a reminder to the speaker that it is time to stop talking. The Timing Call can be used by anyone in the group, providing an opportunity for others in the group to speak. If no one indicates a desire to speak, it is still beneficial for the group to remain silent for a few moments so that everyone can "recover" from the concentration given to the previous speaker and think about the direction they wish the discussion to take. For the person speaking when the Timing Call is requested, there are a number of benefits: she has an opportunity to re-assess the direction her lengthy comments were taking and re-focus on the group as a whole; if she has become somewhat strident, she can take time to calm down.

Calming the Air

Another hand motion that can be used as a signal to the group is a calming motion with both hands, palms down, moving in a slow circular motion. This motion is very helpful for groups that tend to work with a high level of anxiety and stress or who tend to erupt into unproductive Sparking types of discussion. Instead of being helpful to the group, frequent eruptions of everyone talking at once is a signal that anxiety and stress are running amuck. As with the use of the Timing Call, a group can benefit from recognizing this pattern in their interactions and deliberately choosing to take steps to change what happens.

The calming the air motion reminds everyone of their commitment to change interactions that feed unproductive anxieties, and to change to interactions that help everyone remain focused and calm. When someone calms the air, the group can cease the yelling or simultaneous talking, take a deep breath, and remain still while they gather their thoughts and feelings to address what is going on.

Random Ravings

There are times when individuals think of loose ends that were not completely finished during a discussion, or the group leaves a piece of business hanging for lack of clarity on the matter. At some point during the gathering, usually toward the end, loose ends tend to become more obvious. It is helpful to set aside a few moments for everyone to reflect on any items that may need to be mentioned briefly before the group scatters. We call this time on the agenda Random Ravings.[1]

As each woman makes her own notes during the gathering, it is helpful to know that there will be time for addressing Random Ravings. As a reminder, you can circle any note that can be addressed later, and not interrupt the flow of the current discussion. When the time for Random Ravings arrives, a quick review of your notes will help you recall these fleeting thoughts. Also, everyone can scan their notes to see if any loose ends might be dangling that now seem ready to be addressed. If a loose end deserves more discussion, the group can agree to place the item on the agenda for the next gathering.

7

Letting It Happen: Consensus

Consensus is an active commitment to group solidarity and integrity. Arriving at a decision by consensus while taking into account all viewpoints on a given issue, is no easy task. However, it *is* possible. Once you experience decision making by consensus, it is one of the most rewarding and growthful components of a feminist approach to group process.

Consensus within a diverse group is possible because it occurs within the context of the group's purpose and is built consciously to be consistent with the group's Principles of Unity. The consensus-making process also contributes to clarifying and revising the purpose of the group and the Principles of Unity.

Central to Feminist Process is the belief that a group decision reached by consensus is stronger, more valuable, and more lasting than one achieved by a majority, where (sometimes large) minority preferences are not taken into account. A consensus decision is also stronger than any decision made by an individual, no matter how well-informed that individual.

The primary reason that consensus is stronger than traditional methods of decision making is because decisions that affect a group influence everyone's behavior. When everyone has participated in shaping a decision, each individual is able to *act* in concert with that decision because they understand everything that was considered in reaching the decision.

Voting, which sets up a divisive "power-over" dynamic within groups, is not used in the consensus-making process. All opinions, even if only one person brings a particular opinion to the group, are equally valued and carefully considered. As each perspective is considered, it is integrated as an explicit part of the decision, or as a factor that informs the direction the group takes.

Consensus should not be confused with compromise. Compromise focuses on what each person gives up in order to be able to live with a decision. Consensus is a process that focuses on what each person *and* the group as a whole *gain* by the nature of the decision that is reached.

Consensus is not totalitarian "group-think." Unquestioning agreement to a party line is *not* consensus. The group's Principles of Unity provide a common focus for examining diverse views, but are a guide, not dogma. A new viewpoint on an issue can challenge the group to re-examine their Principles of Unity, resulting in healthy growth and change. Individuals usually maintain diverse ideas about an issue, while at the same time taking into account the views of others and the overall sense of the group. Out of this balance grows an ability to willingly move toward a decision that is best for the group.

CALLING FOR CONSENSUS

When all opinions about an issue have been heard (preferably without repetition and reiteration), the Convener or another member of the group summarizes what appears to be the predominant sense of the group and asks if this summary is satisfactory to all who are present. At this point, any alternate viewpoint is expressed and the discussion continues with a focus on reaching a conclusion that takes into account all viewpoints. When there are no new possibilities, consensus has been reached.

Although the process at times seems unending by encouraging full discussion of controversy and differences, the satisfaction that comes from hearing each individual's thoughts and ideas far outweighs the frustrations. If discussion of an issue does not flow easily to decision by consensus, the group can decide not to decide at that time and leave the issue open for discussion later.

Actually, there are very few decisions that cannot wait. Having to decide "not to decide" carries it's own message: more thought and planning need to go into the matter in order to form a sound decision.

If a decision seems urgent and the group is unable to reach consensus, someone needs to call for the group to reflect on how urgent the decision really is. If it is truly not urgent, or if there is an interim decision that can be made, the group leaves the matter open and places it on the agenda for the next gathering. If the decision is urgent, then the group must focus on the necessity of reaching a decision that everyone can live with.

If a decision is still impossible because someone in the group has concerns that cannot be resolved or integrated into a possible decision, the group must take the time to explore with that individual exactly what her concerns are. That individual is responsible for sharing her purposes, objections, and concerns, and exploring in what ways her concerns may be protecting or interfering with the group. Since it is very difficult to be the only one to express a dissenting view within a group, it is the group's responsibility to facilitate this process.

It is not necessary for every member to be present when a decision is made. For most decisions, consensus is reached by those individuals present in a group at the time an issue is discussed. This is possible because the group's Principles of Unity guide the process in a direction with which all members accord. However, if the decision being considered is one that directly affects the work of members of the group who are not present, the decision needs to be considered only as a proposal until all individuals who are directly affected are brought into the discussion. Those present for the discussion are responsible for sharing with those not present the full range of factors considered by the group, either in a written account, audiotape, or discussions with group members. If those who are not present bring new viewpoints to the matter, the group continues the discussion over several gatherings to assure that everyone has the opportunity to participate in the discussion and in the consensus-building process.

TASK GROUPS: GETTING THINGS DONE

There are many circumstances when the *group* (not any individual) delegates responsibilities to a committee, task group, or individual within the group. This is common when there are on-going tasks that require intense work and attention. The group determines what the task group is responsible for and provides guidelines that help that task group accomplish its work in concert with the group's Principles of Unity. The task group then makes decisions and acts in accord with its responsibility. The task group members bring back to the larger group an accounting of their work and issues that require a larger perspective.

One benefit of having task groups for specific or ongoing work is the passing along of skills. A task group usually gets involved in doing intensive work that requires special skills and knowledge. Learning a skill is done by participating in the work, not by simply hearing about the results of the work. Hearing a finance task group's report, no matter how detailed, does not help anyone learn how to balance the books!

Task groups that are most effective in getting the job done *and* in passing along skills are those that have a balance of women who are experienced at the task and those who are learning. This requires a gradual shift over time in who is involved with any task group, so that the work and responsibility rotate.

8

Stepping from Here to There: Closing

Closing is:

- Peace and Power in action.
- Evaluating the group's effectiveness.
- Gaining self-knowledge and knowledge of the group.
- Strengthening communications within the group.
- Focusing on process rather than product.
- Expressing love and respect for individuals and the group.

Closing is a time when every group member shares thoughts and feelings about what has happened during the gathering, and about what they would like to happen next. Each individual's Closing is a three-part statement that includes:

- *Appreciation* for someone or something that has happened during the process of the gathering.
- *Criticism* that brings to the group constructive insights about the processes of the group.
- *Affirmation* that expresses your commitment to moving forward with the group's work and your own individual growth.

It is especially at this time that we:

- Identify and challenge our assumptions.
- Ask critical questions about our values, ideas, and behaviors.

- Examine the context within which events occur.
- Open our Selves to imagining and exploring alternatives for ourselves and for the group.
- Take what we have experienced in the group and begin to form what we want for the future.

Closing is a cohesive element that brings together the individual's intent and commitment and the group's Principles of Unity. The overall goal of Closing is to strengthen the group and each individual.

Even though Closing is the most growthful part of the process, it initially feels quite risky. Often during Closing, feelings that were undercurrents in discussions during the gathering are expressed openly, something we are not accustomed to doing. We often withhold feelings of caring and appreciation because we fear they will be misunderstood or misinterpreted. We typically also repress angry or hurt feelings because they are "not supposed" to be acknowledged openly. In the process of Closing, we express these feelings openly so that everyone in the group can develop a fuller understanding of one another and of the group. When this happens, everyone has the benefit of equal access to knowing what is really going on, internally for individuals, as well as within the group.

THE CLOSING PROCESS

The Closing process is used to close gatherings. It is also used to close a lengthy or intense discussion on a single topic, particularly during a gathering that lasts a day or longer. When the time to Close arrives, the discussion is laid aside and the focus shifts to reflection on the group's process. Commitment to a group using Feminist Process *always* includes commitment to Closing. It is crucial that all individuals who are present at a gathering be fully *Present* for Closing.

Closing is *always* on the agenda. Sometimes groups, especially in the early stages of getting established, or when time is consumed with decision making, are tempted to skip Closing. This is *most* unwise! Time is reserved for this component to occur as the last item on the agenda, usually just after Random Ravings. For a one-hour gathering, at least 10 minutes should be devoted to Closing. For a half-day or longer gathering, allow 30 minutes to an hour. At the agreed upon time, the group takes a few minutes for each person to reflect on what has happened during the discussion and to review her notes. Each group member then shares her appreciation, criticism, and affirmation.

Appreciation

This part of Closing acknowledges something that someone did or said, or a group interaction, that you appreciate. This is a time to actively nurture one another and your work by sharing your ideas about specific ways in which you and the group benefited from something that happened. For example, if someone's comment in the discussion was a turning point to help clarify an issue for you, or moved the group discussion to a different level, you would state your appreciation for the comment and share with the group how or why this comment was so important to you and the group.

An appreciation that has the following elements will help you and others in the group build on what has just happened:

- The names of individuals who are responsible for what it is you appreciate.
- A brief description of their specific acts or behavior.
- Sharing what this means to you.
- Your ideas about what this means in terms of the group's Principles of Unity.

Criticism

Criticism, in a feminist context of love and respect is critical, precise, thoughtful reflection/action directed toward transformation. It is a tool for becoming aware of actions and behaviors that maintain an unjust and sexist society. When criticism is used with commitment to feminist values, it becomes a powerful tool for reaching agreement on what will be done and why, and how individuals can relate in order to create a future that we envision. By working through disagreements and doubts, a group is better able to remain united and can continue to work together when the going gets tough.

Criticism, as we traditionally know the term, raises fears of being judged harshly or unfavorably, or being unfairly assigned qualities or intentions that are not our own. We use the term criticism for this component of Closing because of the positive connotations that it carries in the Arts, where developing your art to its finest level depends upon your own and others' criticisms. This type of criticism identifies the meanings of your work and reveals what creative possibilities could be further developed.

The art critic brings to the art insights and interpretations that help others to appreciate more fully what the artist has done, and what the art means for the culture as a whole. The critic does not proclaim the "correct" view of the art, but does provide a well-informed, knowledgeable interpretation of the art that helps others understand the art better, even if they don't agree with the views of the critic.

Constructive and effective criticism in a feminist context is like that of a well-developed art criticism. It brings to the group the best that each of us has to offer, with the intent of helping everyone in the group better understand what we are all about. Here is a way to frame your criticism that will enable you to claim ownership of your concerns and provide specific content that will make a criticism clear. A growthful and constructive criticism[1] includes:

- I am . . . (your own feeling about what has happened).
- When . . . (a specific action, behavior, or circumstance that is the focus of your thinking).
- I want . . . (specific changes you want to happen).
- Because . . . (how your ideas connect with the group's Principles of Unity).

Affirmation

The conclusion of the three-step process of Closing is a statement of affirmation that gives the group a sense of the way in which you are working to grow as an individual and as a member of the group.

Affirmations are simple statements that speak to our deeper Selves. They concentrate our energy on the healing, growthful aspects of our work together. They are a powerful tool for creating change and growth in a direction that we desire.[2]

An affirmation reflects a reality that is not yet fully a part of your life, but it is stated as if it has already come about. Affirmations offered during Closing grow out of your experiences in the group, and often are related to your specific appreciations and criticisms. They also come from the internal work you do apart from the group. For example, at a time when you feel uncertain about a decision, your affirmation might be: "I trust my own inner sense and the wisdom of our group." When you are disturbed by a conflict, an affirmation to help transform the conflict might be: "I reside in the care that we have for each other (Adair, 1984, p.46)."

Initially it is difficult to affirm yourself. Until you are comfortable creating your own, use an affirmation that someone else suggests. As your sense of self-affirmation grows, you will create your own. As you become accustomed to using affirmations as a source of directing your energy to create change, you will become skilled at expressing an affirmation during Closing that moves you and the group from the circumstances of the present into a future you choose and create.

An affirmation is characterized by the following:

- It is a positive and simple statement.
- It is stated in the present tense.
- It is grounded in your present reality, but also provides a bridge to the future you seek.

HOW-TO, HELPFUL HINTS, AND HOMEWORK

Because Closing is of such major importance, the following sections provide more detailed explanations and suggestions.

Getting Your Head and Heart Together

Getting ready to participate in Closing requires thoughtful reflection so that you are clear about the content of what you want to say before you speak. Once you are clear about the content of your three-part Closing statement, it is possible to state it briefly and simply.

Most of us have not learned to share our own responses to situations while we are in the situation, and so this does not come easily or naturally. Practice is important. Even more important is a supportive, aware group that is fully committed to each individual's growth.

Written notes that you have taken throughout the gathering become crucial at the time of Closing. Productive gatherings are rarely placid! In the intensity of the discussion, you are likely to have thoughts and feelings about *what* happened and *how* it was being done. Perhaps your perspective has shifted now that the discussion has ended. You may have become aware of an insight and are now beginning to get clear within. To help get clearer about your thoughts, ask yourself:

- Did I *Do* what I *Know*—were my behaviors consistent with my values and with our Principles of Unity?
- Were my actions honestly motivated by love and respect for myself, others, and the group?
- Did I remain tuned in and aware or did I check-out mentally at some point?
- Am I aware of conflicts or differences that still need to be addressed?
- What occurred that promoted my own individual growth and the growth of the group?
- What changes would I like to make in my behavior?[3]

Being Specific about the Agent

One of the powers of patriarchal culture depends on obscuring responsibility for events and actions. (See Chapter 2.) Sometimes owning responsibility can be uncomfortable because we regret what we are doing or have done. Often it is difficult to own responsibility because of shyness or false modesty. Sometimes we may feel a misguided concern about protecting a "confidence." Sometimes we are hesitant to name someone specifically because of fear that they will be personally offended or embarrassed. Sometimes our discomfort comes from a general sense of something that has not been clearly thought through.

Naming an instance and an agent(s) (especially when the agent is yourself) is critical for growth to occur. Being obscure and mystifying a concern creates a lack of trust, suspicion, and divisiveness. Naming the agent helps everyone in the group to understand more about the context of the issues. It makes it possible to move forward to build trust and trustworthiness between members of the group.[4]

Consider the following examples:

> *Mystifying statement:* "The checkbook ledger has been well maintained for the past few months. This will make taxes much easier to prepare this year." Although everyone in the group may know who has been keeping the checkbook lately, and who is going to prepare taxes, this statement discounts the individuals and makes them anonymous. It creates divisiveness because of the implied message that someone before had not done a good job of keeping the checkbook (which may not be at all what you are referring to, or which may not be true).

> *Demystifying statement:* "Anne, you have done a wonderful job of keeping the checkbook. I appreciate how much this will help me in getting taxes prepared this year." This statement lets everyone in the group know how well Anne, specifically, has been doing her job of keeping the checkbook balanced. It carries the message that Anne has a skill that others might want to know about. It lets everyone know that you own the responsibility for getting taxes prepared, and that you see your task as dependent upon the work that others are doing. The focus on the present situation effectively erases the implied mystifying message about what happened in the past.

> *Mystifying statement:* "I can't stand all this clutter!" Here you are owning the fact that you see the clutter and

that you are irritated. The mystification and divisiveness in this statement arise from the fact that each person in the group begins to wonder if you are irritated with her clutter, specifically, or what she might have done to bring on this outburst. The matter of the clutter becomes only a vehicle for expressing your irritation, which may be irritation with the clutter, but it also could be irritation with a person. This lack of clarity breeds distrust, suspicion, and divisive power-over relations.

Demystifying statement: "I am irritated with this clutter. I am not sure who is responsible, but it seems to me that it is worse after Jane, Becky, and Joan have been here for their publicity meeting. Maybe we need more space to store their art supplies. Or, maybe we are all just getting careless about leaving things around. I am willing to help work out a solution. What do other people think?" Here the fact that you are not sure about who is responsible is stated, and your uncertainty is more believable because you go on to identify a group who may be contributing more than others. You are also offering a possible solution, and stating your intention to help solve the problem. This leaves you accessible to the group in the event that they find your compulsion over clutter irritating! There is no room for suspicion, and the level of trust and cohesiveness can build within the group because of the message that "we are in this together."

Being Specific about Your Feelings and Your Observations

A feeling statement is a precise communication of what is happening within yourself. It carries no hidden messages about what anyone else has done or is doing. An observation statement is a clear description of what you or someone else has done or said. An observation does not include what you think another person meant or what you suppose they intended.

Since it is risky to own and communicate feelings, the tendency is to infer something about what someone else is doing or saying. There is a vast difference between labeling a woman "arrogant" and owning your own feelings of jealousy and competitiveness because she is good at what she does. Being clear about your feelings encourages you to take ownership of your feelings and avoids blaming or "guilt-tripping" another person. It lets the other person(s) know what is going on with you in such a way that you are accessible. Compare the following statements:

> *Interpretive/blaming statement:* "I feel rejected because I am never included in things." Even though the word "feel" is used, this statement avoids your own feelings of hurt and implies that someone has behaved with the intent of rejecting you. You may think someone has rejected you because of something that happened, but your feeling is anger, hurt, or fear, regardless of the intention or behavior of the other person.

> *Constructive statement:* "I am angry because I didn't know about the change in our meeting time." This statement communicates exactly what you are experiencing, states a fact about what has happened, and can lead to a constructive response. The response might clarify a misunderstanding: "I was disappointed that you weren't at the meeting. I expected that you would be there because I left a message tucked in your door on Tuesday afternoon. In the future, I will make sure that I get the information to you directly."

> *Interpretive/blaming statement:* "Sue, you are so irresponsible. You are always late." This statement inappropriately assigns a personality trait to Sue. Being labeled "irresponsible" puts Sue in a box without any openings. Your statement is a judgment that merely intimidates Sue and everyone else in the group and creates divisiveness.

> *Constructive statement:* "Sue, I am irritated because you have been 30 minutes late for the last four meetings. This is disruptive to the group. Do we need to reconsider the schedule?" This statement clearly communicates

what you are feeling and identifies the behavior that you have observed and how it affects the group. The group members can all enter into a problem-solving discussion. Sue can then address what circumstances in her life have led to her being late, or she can accept the suggestion that the group change the meeting time.

Stating What You Want

When giving criticism directed toward something that needs to be done or that needs to change, provide a clear, specific statement of what you want. It is important to focus on what you *do* want. Stating what you want is not a demand, nor does it mean that the group will respond by giving you what you want! What it does is to move the group toward a solution or toward a constructive response to your criticism. If your criticism turns out not to fit for others in the group, the group can sort that out and still attend to your concern as fitting for you.

Typical habits of patriarchal culture lead to two tendencies: stating what we don't want or merely implying what we want with some indirect or nonspecific comment. Compare the effectiveness of each of the following statements:

> *Constructive statement of what you want:* "I want two women to help with this project."

> *Saying what you don't want:* "I don't think we should have too many women on this project."

> *Implying what you want indirectly:* "People in this group just aren't willing to get involved."

Responding to Appreciation and to Criticism

The most difficult thing to learn about both appreciation and criticism is how to take them. No matter how well-delivered, it is not easy to hear either appreciations or criticisms, especially in front of a group.

When you receive an appreciation, you have the following responsibilities:

1. Remain in an active listening mode while the person who is sharing the appreciation has completed her thoughts. Do not interrupt her or respond directly to her. Appreciation is shared not only for you to hear, but for the entire group to learn and grow from. Your response would interrupt this process.

2. Most often you need only to listen actively. If you do respond verbally in the group, graciously accept the appreciation. Our socialization encourages habits of discounting compliments or putting them down in some way. We tend to say things like "Oh, it was nothing," or "I could have done it better." These responses discount the person who has shared her appreciation and detract from the growthful effect that the appreciation, as well as your own actions, could have for the entire group.

When you receive a criticism, you have at least four responsibilities:

1. Make sure you understand clearly what the criticism is. This usually means that your first verbal response, if any, is to paraphrase what you perceive the criticism to be.

2. Wait to hear the perspectives of others in the group. Usually different people have different perceptions of a situation, and hearing these will help you decide how well the criticism "fits."

3. Weigh within yourself the validity of the criticism or how fair or accurate you think it is. Sometimes you will know immediately that the criticism is fair. More often, you will need from few minutes to several days to reflect on the criticism and integrate it.

4. Respond in a constructive manner. For a valid and fair criticism, the most constructive response is a behavioral response—you take the criticism to heart and change your behavior! If you decide that the criticism is not fair, share your thoughts with the group.

It is difficult to respond to criticism without defensiveness or apology and often we don't even recognize when we are doing it. Defenses or apologies do not contribute to the growth of the group, yourself, or other individuals. Compare the following responses:

Constructive response: "I think that you are right, Jane. I will work on this during the coming week and would like to have people tell me how they perceive what I am doing." Or, if you think there is an element of unfairness about the criticism: "I think that Jane has not taken into account the fact I depend on public transportation."

Defensive response: "I think that Jane is right but I was working as hard as I could to get this task completed." Or, "Give me a break. I'm doing the best I can." If you think that the group has not recognized the work that you have put into the task, then share this thought with the group but focus on what you are feeling and thinking about your future behavior in relation to the criticism.

Apology: "I know that Jane is right and I am very sorry. What more can I say?" There is a lot more that you can say—and do. Being sorry does not make things right nor does it help you or the group move forward. If you feel regretful about what happened, share your feeling of regret and indicate what you and the group can learn from the situation.

Putting It All Together

In describing suggestions of "how-to" say things well in sharing a criticism, it is easy to lose sight of how this works together in a group. The following situation provides an example of a criticism given at the end of a gathering, when Justa became increasingly aware of the ageist implications of a remark she made in response to Adrienne, a younger woman in the group. At the time of Closing, Justa shared her criticism: "I am uncomfortable because of the comment I made to Adrienne earlier: 'When you are older,

Adrienne, you will understand.' I want to examine my own ageism because I am committed to creating a safe space here and think my remark was divisive and obstructive in contributing to that, not only for Adrienne, but for others as well."

At first, Adrienne did not respond. Two other women in the group "made nice" and tried to reassure Justa that her remark was not ageist. They thought the remark indicated Justa's desire to "help" Adrienne. Other women in the group shared their perceptions that confirmed the ageist implications of the remark.

After thoughtful reflection and hearing others' perceptions, Adrienne was able to tune in to her own sense. She shared with the group that she felt angry when she heard the remark, but her awareness at the time had only been partial. Her immediate response had been to "scold" herself internally and to rationalize that Justa meant well and, therefore, she "should" not have those negative feelings. She acknowledged that without the group's focus, she would have left the gathering with a sense of distance from Justa, a sense of not belonging to the group, most of whom were older than herself, and discounting her own reality. Now that it had been addressed openly, she was able to acknowledge what had happened and assist the group in examining the meaning of the incident. Once Adrienne focused the group's attention on *her* reality, everyone's awareness of ageism and its divisiveness increased by leaps and bounds.

Criticism as Homework

Sometimes we are able to think clearly and speak artfully at the time of Closing. Often, we can only do so after we have left the group and have done our own internal work at home, especially when it comes to criticism. When you sense that there is a criticism you need to develop at home, indicate during Closing the nature of your concern, and ask the group to wait for a fuller criticism at the next gathering, either during Check-In or as an agenda item.

Artful criticism is given at a time when the group is receptive, open, and ready to address the concerns in the criticism. You may need to wait for a time that is right or to ask the group to plan for a time that can be set aside to address the issue.

Artful criticism arises from our deepest feelings, is energized by our emotions, and is finely crafted by our clearest thinking. It is shared with others in a manner and at a time when full awareness (including thoughts and feelings) can be called upon to address the issue. The homework that is required to do this includes getting in touch with the full range of feelings that you experience around the issue, and thinking about all of the facts and circumstances that are a part of the situation. It requires thinking through similar circumstances that you have experienced to search for a perspective that comes from that broader experience, and envisioning future possibilities that might emerge from this experience.

Constructive criticism is placed in the context of the purposes of the group. One way to do this is to take time to review the group's Principles of Unity. Think about the present situation in light of each Principle and how the group can be strengthened by addressing the issue you are studying.

The homework of criticism involves carefully weighing possibilities; possibilities for what might be different in a similar circumstance in the future, as well as possibilities for what might now emerge from the situation as it is. Mentally imagine how you and the group might move forward in a direction that you carefully choose rather than a direction that just happens.

As you reflect on the situation, write ideas and thoughts on a sheet of paper. You can go over these notes to sort out which of your ideas are beneficial and constructive and re-think ideas that may not be constructive. Once you see your ideas on paper, you can explore different ways of saying things, and make sure everything you need to say is there. When you share your ideas with the group, the notes you prepare at home can help you to remain focused, and include your full range of feelings and thoughts, stated in constructive and beneficial ways.

Creating Affirmations

Affirmations often grow out of internal work that we do apart from the group, as well as our experiences in the group. This work involves shifting our attention away from frustrations and problems to possibilities for growth and change. As you reflect on these possibilities, you will begin to form affirmations that provide a message to your inner consciousness that you are receptive to the energy of change moving in a creative, healing direction.

Since the inner consciousness is responsive to repetition, it is important to repeat affirmations to yourself, using the same wording again and again (with shifts in the wording as you find what is most comfortable for you). Repeat the affirmations while you are doing rhythmic activities, such as exercising, cleaning, or walking. When you re-enter the group, you will bring with you the deep inner resources that you have developed within yourself to more effectively participate in the group.

Here are some examples:

- I value the light and clarity that I bring to situations.[5]
- All that I know is available to me when I need it.
- I believe in myself and our group.
- I care for my Self.
- I am at peace with those I love.
- I am in tune with my intuition.
- I believe in the power of our group.
- I act with confidence in my ability.
- I am nourished by the love we share for each other.
- I willingly release the old and welcome the new in my life.
- I choose wisely because I listen to my inner voice.
- I gladly accept the support of those with whom I work.
- My love for myself brings love and support to all my relationships.

9

Valuing Diversity and Unity: Conflict Transformation

Your group values diversity if . . .

- You can name at least *one* thing your group does during every meeting that reflects the valuing of each individual equally.
- You can identify at least *two* recent occasions when your group's decisions took into account the minority view.
- You can describe at least *three* Principles of Unity held in common by each member of your group.
- You can name at least *four* recent occasions when the leadership in your group shifted spontaneously in response to the issue under discussion.
- You can identify (in your group's most recent meeting) at least *five* instances when members freely expressed appreciation for one another.
- You can describe at least two points of conflict that your group is currently considering;

And, for each of the two points, you can describe at least three distinctly different perspectives that are being considered by the group.

In Chapter 2, we describe the Power of Diversity as encouraging creativity, valuing alternative views and encouraging flexibility; and the Power of Unity as valuing thoughtful deliberation about and integration of variety within the group. Even at the best of times, none of us are consistently able to behaviorally enact these powers to our full satisfaction or to the well-being of the group. When we cannot integrate diversity or variety, we say that we are engaged in conflict. Typically we deal with conflict by ignoring it, backing away from it, getting caught up in it, or "agreeing to disagree."

In order to move beyond those typical patterns of dealing with conflict, it is important to examine common definitions of conflict and come to fresh understandings of how patriarchal bias influences our thinking. Once we have a fresh perspective, we can then move on to enacting the Power of Diversity and the Power of Unity, and embrace conflict as an opportunity for growth and an important part of group experience. Openly and consciously addressing conflict is one of the most important steps toward creating unity and toward valuing diversity in group interactions.

RE-DEFINING CONFLICT

Patriarchal definitions of the word "conflict" refer to incompatibility, opposing action, antagonism, and hostility.[1] Underlying those definitions is the suggestion of the potential for violence. Given how we learn language, all of those connotations are immediately known to us at some level—little wonder that conflict is something we would prefer to avoid!

In fact, conflict is *not* always the same thing as hostility, antagonism, or incompatibility. This is not to say that hostility cannot exist between two people or within a group. A simple disagreement can quickly escalate into something that carries feelings of enmity, the polarization of viewpoints into "right and wrong," and hostility.

A number of traditional approaches to dealing with conflict might be effective (conflict resolution, negotiation, arbitration), but these approaches focus on reducing hostilities and on an outcome of compromise between opposing groups or individuals. They do not *transform* conflict itself.

A first step in moving toward a reality where conflict is valued and valuable is to recognize the limits of patriarchal definitions about conflict and to create a new way of thinking about conflict. There is no word in American English to express the peaceful, even welcomed co-existence of differing points of view, different perspectives, or different ideas about how things are to be done. When there are several opinions about an issue that reflect disagreement and where the disagreement matters to the work of the group, honest discussion can proceed without hostility, antagonism, or competition for being "right." However, even when there is hostility, antagonism, or competition, it is possible to transform conflict of all types into something beneficial for the group and for the individuals in it. Being able to do this depends on knowing that you have a *choice* in dealing with conflict, and that you *can* learn ways to transform conflict, in addition to reducing or eliminating hostility and antagonism.

FOUNDATIONS FOR TRANSFORMING CONFLICT INTO UNITY AND DIVERSITY

It is not possible to transform conflict by waiting until conflict happens and *then* begin to work on ways to deal with it differently. There are three important things that groups can do during times of relative calm that build a strong foundation for transforming conflict. These are:

- *Nurturing a strong sense of rotating leadership within the group.* A group that has practiced Rotating Chair will be able to turn to those who have the clarity, vision, and energy to address the conflict (see Chapters 5 and 6). When conflict occurs, leadership that can focus the group's attention and provide some clear guidance in staying focused is a critical element to bringing about transformation. If every individual within a group has experience at being a leader, each person already feels strong and supported in her leadership role, and can comfortably move into this role when the group does experience conflict.

- *Practicing constructive criticism.* Criticism (see Chapter 8) provides a way to move out of communication styles of blaming, reinforcing hostile interactions, and personalizing issues. Instead, members of the group develop communication skills that focus on the group's responsibility for what happens in the group, and on future possibilities for constructive growth and change. Practice in using constructive criticism builds clarity about the group's Principles of Unity so that when conflict occurs, this clarity can be used as a resource for addressing the conflict.

- *Practicing ways to value diversity.* If your group has established habits of being together that draw you closer toward valuing individual differences, then when you do experience conflict you will have a strong basis from which to transform the conflict. The processes of Check-In (see Chapter 5) and Closing (see Chapter 8) are two ways for groups to recognize the diversity that exists within the group. Review the list of items at the beginning of this chapter for specific suggestions as to how to evaluate your group's willingness to value diversity.

INDIVIDUAL APPROACHES THAT TRANSFORM CONFLICT

Conflict within a group is a group responsibility; however, each individual can take significant steps toward changing patterns of behavior and communication that contribute to conflict, as well as for dealing with conflict. There are three approaches to individual change that we have found particularly helpful:

- The gentle art of verbal self-defense,
- Reclaiming the virtues of gossip, and
- Anger as a source of strength.

The Gentle Art of Verbal Self-Defense

Suzette Haden Elgin has developed a system of language behavior that is simple to learn and that creates dramatic shifts in interaction patterns.[2] We recommend her suggestions because they are specially designed to reduce hostility in human interactions and, in turn, improve both individual and group well-being. Using the gentle art of verbal self-defense makes it possible to get out of negative loops of hostile verbal interactions and move instead into language that opens the way for greater understanding of differences.

A common hostile interaction involves a cycle of blaming and counterblaming—a loop that can be interrupted by shifting to a response that does not feed the loop of blame. An example of a hostile, blaming statement is: "If you REALly CARED about this GROUP, you would keep your PROBlems to yourSELF." A response that feeds the hostility and blame is the familiar "WHO do you think YOU are to act as if YOU never bring YOUR problems to this GROUP." A response that would interrupt the loop would be "It is interesting to consider that people's problems influence group interaction." This is a "computer mode" response that does not blame anyone; it moves away from the hostility and sends the clear message "I am not going to participate in a negative interaction." Unlike more familiar responses of simply ignoring the blamer, or walking away from the situation, responses that effectively interrupt a negative or hostile verbal interaction also send the message "I will stay and talk, but I will not do so in a way that hurts."

The gentle art of verbal self-defense is accessible and possible to learn even in less than ideal circumstances. You can work with any of the books[2] on your own, or you can work with others in your group to practice the language behaviors in your group. You will find that even one or two shifts in how you habitually respond to hostility will create dramatic changes in your verbal interactions, making it possible to experience conflict in ways that move far beyond the hostility.

Reclaiming the Virtues of Gossip

Talk outside the group about people and events in the group, commonly known as gossip, can be a destructive source of group conflict or it can be an important source of group energy. Gossip is a skill that is linked with women's talk.[3] Gossip, like many other words in the English language that refer primarily to women, once had a positive meaning that has now been distorted to a negative meaning. Originally, the word "gossip" was a noun for the woman who assisted the midwife at the time of birth. The "gossip" was the labor coach, and after the birth she went into the community to spread the news about the birth. She was considered a very wise woman who could communicate the wisdom of the stars.[4]

We can reclaim the art of gossip.[5] Doing so makes it possible to envision new possibilities for how we talk about one another and events in a group. The talk shared among group members in the less structured setting outside the group can be an important source of energy that, like the labor coach, helps to give birth to the ideas and visions of the group. The "ethics of gossip" that follow build on the feminist values of *Peace and Power* and reclaim the virtues of gossip:

- Gossip is to be purposeful. When you tell a story about someone or something, tell why you are sharing the story. For example, if you are telling your friend about a budding sexual involvement between two members of the group, share that the reason you are passing along this information is because of your concerns for the sensitivity of the situation in the group, and that you are seeking ways to interrupt the divisiveness that could result.

- Own your Self. Focus on your own feelings and ideas, rather than what you think someone else felt or thought. Even though you may be concerned about how other people in the group may feel or react to the emerging sexual involvement referred to above, focus your gossip on how *you* feel about it, and what your thoughts are about how it may contribute to divisiveness in the group.

- Name your source. When passing along information, be clear about how you came by the information. Share who told you about what happened, or how you know about what happened. Do not say, for example, "the committee decided to deny your petition." If you were not there when the committee made this decision, indicate how you know about the decision: "Nancy, who chairs the committee, has told me that the committee denied your petition." If you were there, say: "I was present when the committee voted to deny your petition, and I was one of the people who voted to deny because . . . "

- Be cautious about presenting information in such a way that could be used to hurt another person; give information in a way that opens possibilities for greater compassion and understanding. For example, information that could be hurtful would be to leave a class saying: "I was astonished at what Priscilla said in class today! She really is intolerant!" A message that could convey the same astonishment, but not misrepresent or label Priscilla, would be: "I was astonished when I heard Priscilla's views on the militarization of women's lives. I need to think through how to continue this discussion the next time we meet."

- Affirm the opportunity and possibility for growth and change. When talking about Priscilla's comments on militarization, examine various points that you think need to be explored to move the discussion toward constructive understanding. Gossip that focuses on what else needs to happen moves toward greater understanding of the issues.

- Use humor as a way to address emotions and to shed light on a situation. Be very cautious about hurtful, diminishing teasing. Never knowingly tease or ridicule another person and be cautious about humor that is self-denigrating. For example, a comment made with a laughing tone: "I guess I am just an unimportant student who has no business expressing my opinion" is not funny, nor is it dry humor. It is self-denigrating, and it passively implies ridicule of others about whose opinions you are only speculating.

- Use information to share and inform, not to manipulate. For example, if you honestly think that your friend is doing something wrong, then provide to her *all* the information you can, without prodding or coercing her decision in the direction you desire. Leave the decision to her, even if it may turn out to be one with which you do not agree.

- Use gossip to assist and to build community, not to compete. When you hear another woman's story, stay away from responding with a "one-up" story of your own. Instead, focus on sharing ideas and feelings as to what her story means to you and how, together, you can learn from the story. For example, if a friend tells you about a terrible thing that has happened at work when pay raises were given, do not launch into your own "ain't it awful" story about when you were denied a pay raise. You may indicate that you have had an experience that is similar, but keep the focus of the discussion on what your friend has experienced and is learning about the politics of her work life.

Anger as a Source of Strength

Anger is something that many women have learned to deny, either as a feeling they can own or that they have a right to own. Understandably, women have learned to fear the anger of others because it is so closely linked to life-threatening violence against women. We have even learned that our own anger can elicit life-threatening violence against us, further enforcing our fear of our own anger. Like the word conflict, anger is a word that is used in Western societies to cover a great many feelings and dynamics in human relationships. While there is a fundamental feeling we know as "anger," there are other feelings and dynamics that acquire the label as well. Anger is not the same thing as hatred, dislike, violence, or envy. Because we cannot readily distinguish the differences between these types of feelings, we have few resources to respond differently or appropriately to protect ourselves, or to use our feelings in a healthy way. It is little wonder that we have difficulty in dealing with anger even in groups where we know that there is some measure of safety.

In groups that are committed to shifting ways of working with one another, dealing constructively with anger is a major step toward creating the safety needed to deal with conflict. Things that we have found helpful in learning new ways to deal with anger are:

- Realize that your anger (real anger, not hatred or violence) is a valuable tool or clue that something different needs to happen. Learn to take the time to move away from the situation until you are clear about what needs to happen differently. Use your anger as a signal to step away from the situation until you think through exactly what needs to change.

- Realize that confrontation is usually not a constructive approach to dealing with anger; instead confrontation usually polarizes and distances you from other people involved in the situation. Once you take the time to get clear about the "signal" that your anger represents, then you can think through approaches that address the situation directly and calmly, moving toward constructive changes in the situation.[6] Giving constructive criticism (see Chapter 8) is one way to do this, providing an opportunity to own your feeling of anger and communicating clearly what you want to happen next and why.

- Find ways to work with your anger in safe ways with other people who can support your growth, and who understand what you are working on. Doing so will help you overcome your fear of anger, so that it no longer immobilizes you but becomes a source of strength.

GROUP APPROACHES TO TRANSFORMING CONFLICT

Whenever conflict enters the awareness of the group as a whole, or individuals within the context of the group, it is group conflict. It is always tempting to dismiss conflict as "personality differences" and advise the two or three individuals to work it out somewhere outside of the group. While it is indeed desirable for individuals to resolve differences in peaceful ways outside the group, conflict or hostile interactions within the group require a group response if it is to be transformative *for* the group.

Group conflict is no *one* person's responsibility; no one or two individuals can resolve group conflict even if they resolve conflict between themselves. Group conflict is *everyone's* responsibility. The outcome of openly dealing with conflict is *transformation* where every individual learns, gains new insights, and experiences new possibilities. It is only when conflict is addressed in a group that many differing points of view can be taken in, because many different people speak to the issue at hand. Rather than having to resolve two points of view of individuals who are "at odds" in a group, several different people speak to the issue and many more possibilities emerge. The rich exchange that happens in this process illuminates the diversity that exists among group members and provides the insights from which awareness of common ground emerges.

The process that we describe involves three distinct group actions that bring about transformation of conflict. These are:

- Owning group conflict.
- Ending habits that sustain divisiveness.
- Finding a unifying value and exploring diversity.

Owning Group Conflict

When conflict occurs in a group, it is often initially expressed as if it were a conflict between two individuals, or between two opposing "factions" within the group. By isolating the opposing individuals or factions within the group by labeling the conflict as simply "their issue," we fail to recognize and own the conflict for what it is—a group conflict. An alternative is to move the discussion toward group ownership of the conflict, bringing to group consciousness diverse points of view and possibilities for reaching new understandings. In the process of claiming group ownership of a conflict, the misunderstandings of the conflict are brought to light, each individual sees her own actions from the fresh perspective that comes from group wisdom, and real shifts in attitude and in action can begin to flow.

For example, Chullie, Justa, Lynn, Sue, and Betty form a writers' support group and decide to meet weekly over the summer. Chullie and Justa are the most experienced writers in the group and the other women often turn to them for guidance. One of their Principles of Unity is to equalize the balance of power among them through sharing information and through valuing each person's contributions to the work of the group. Over the course of several weeks, Justa becomes aware that whenever Lynn asks a question, it is directed only at her; when Justa speaks, Lynn pays careful attention and when others speak Lynn appears disinterested; when Lynn does talk in the group, she looks only at Justa and always manages to sit where she can maintain eye contact with Justa. Not having yet reached full awareness of all the underlying issues, Justa is very uncomfortable with what she perceives as "shero-worship." During Closing at one gathering, Justa shares her (as yet imperfect) awareness with the group in her criticism of Lynn's behavior and its affect on her. She states that what she wants to happen is a more equal interaction between Lynn and other members of the group.

At Check-In the following week, Betty responds to Justa's criticism by saying that she thinks the issue between Lynn and Justa is merely a "personality conflict" and that Justa has a personal sensitivity about her status as a successful writer that the group needs to explore. Chullie indicates that she feels Lynn's admiration of Justa is interfering with the work of the group and suggests that the group needs to look at how each person is contributing to the interactions between Justa and Lynn. Sue does not speak to the issue. Lynn begins to cry and denies that she is treating Justa differently than she treats anyone else. After several exchanges that move the group further into confusion and misunderstandings, they agree to meet again later that week to look only at this issue and to place tasks "on hold" until the conflict can be resolved.

While their Principle of Unity reflects the ideal that members of this group are seeking better ways to work together, they have encountered a conflict that could remain isolated as an issue between two people and continue to plague the effective working relationships within the group. By the time of the meeting to discuss the conflict, Justa had taken time to reflect on what she had noticed about Lynn's behavior and her own responses to it, and carefully reframed a criticism that focused on how their behavior had excluded the others in the group. Sue moved into a leadership role and prepared a SOPHIA that consciously refocused the group's awareness on their Principle of Unity: "We will seek to equalize the balance of power among us"; she offered several ideas she thought would more fully enact this principle. Chullie shared her awareness that Justa often speaks eloquently to the topic of discussion, but does not facilitate other people expressing their point of view. Betty, who has not noticed any of these dynamics, shared that the open expression of the conflict had given her the awareness that she had continued to feel like a real novice in the group and that she now realized, this feeling was keeping her relatively unempowered as a writer. Lynn, who sincerely had not intended to treat Justa differently, began to realize that by deferring to Justa she had unconsciously sustained a power dynamic that she indeed found distasteful, but did not know how to interrupt. Additionally, she recognized that she had not noticed the particular skills that Sue and Chullie also brought to the group, and had assumed that Betty was there, like herself, merely to learn how to write from the one person she recognized as an expert.

Once the group had entered into a full discussion of their perspectives, several things happened. Lynn consciously interrupted her doting behavior and asked the group's feedback and support for acting on her intention to sustain mutually respectful relationships with everyone in the group. Justa realized that she felt a certain "performance anxiety" to always provide answers and was relieved to be able to relax and interact just as any other group member. She had not been aware that her ready answers were not allowing others to contribute and reframed her affirmation to honor other women's contributions before assuming she had the only relevant answers. Betty gained a new appreciation for a talent she had not previously realized that she had in the area of proof-reading and accurate spelling. She made a commitment to the group to bring these skills to the process of the group. Sue and Chullie gained a new respect for their own leadership skills and ability to stay with an uncomfortable situation until it was thoroughly explored.

In this example, the key to transforming the conflict was to own the conflict as a group problem. If the group had continued to isolate the problem as existing between Justa and Lynn, nothing new could have happened. In fact, the same old patterns of hurt feelings, continued aggravation, and frustration would have persisted. In first owning, and then transforming the conflict, each individual gained new insights about her unique strengths; each individual also gained self-knowledge of ways she could grow.

This group truly moved toward honoring diversity within the group, while at the same time growing in awareness of the unifying value upon which their diversity rests.

Ending Habits That Sustain Divisiveness

Divisiveness is an all-too familiar experience among groups. Divisiveness obscures our commonalities, side-tracking us from our expressed desire to value unity and diversity. Most of the things that sustain divisiveness in groups are habits that we have learned as the "right" or "savvy" or "political" way to deal with group conflict. In fact, these habits are rooted in patriarchal values where the individual is assumed to be at odds with the group and with other individuals in the group, and where integrating differences is not conceived as a possibility, much less a value. The following list shows examples of many such behaviors, contrasted with behaviors or actions that would be an alternative leading to a valuing of diversity in groups.

Individual behaviors that reflect your contributions toward a group's valuing of diversity and divisiveness:

Diversity	*Divisiveness*

When I am convinced that my point of view is the only reasonable one:

I still take the time to find out what other people think.	I keep repeating it to make sure that everyone hears it.

When things become tense in a discussion, and "sides are being drawn":

I try to encourage discussion so that each point of view is fully presented.	I usually know what side I am on and grow impatient with drawn out discussions.

In a meeting:

I make sure I express my point of view and limit my comments so that others may also speak to the issue.	I make sure I express my point of view at length so that others don't miss out on the relevance of my insights.

Diversity	*Divisiveness*

When I am aware that something I have said or done has bothered someone:

| I stop to consider what has happened and try to put myself in her shoes. | I figure it is her problem and it is up to her to work it out. |

When others are expressing their views:

| I actively listen and hear them out before framing my response. | I usually already know what they are trying to say and jump in to say what I have to say to move the discussion along. |

When there is disagreement in the group:

| I invite each person to express her viewpoint so that we can all hear and take it into account in reaching a decision. | I think the best way to deal with it is simply to agree to disagree. |

When I am unable to attend a scheduled meeting:

| I make sure someone knows my concerns about relevant issues and is willing to take them to the group. | I figure most meetings are a waste of my time and I prefer not to attend anyway. |

Establishing a Unifying Value and Exploring Diversity

A key to conflict transformation is finding what value (or values) brings the group together, and then identifying the unifying value from which the conflict emerges. This is not easy to do. Often, the conflict itself is named in such a way that the unifying value is obscured. However, we have yet to experience a group conflict where there is no possible unifying value. When conflict occurs, something about the conflict matters to the members of the group in a significant way. If the issue did not matter, there would be no conflict. The process of figuring out the unifying value underlying the conflict, or why it matters so much to the members of the group, always reveals better understandings of the differences that exist. With the unifying value before the group, the members of the group can explore ways to value their diversity within the framework of the unifying value.

As an example, a "conflict" that is common among feminist groups involves different perspectives on the question: "What is feminism?" This question will never be "answered" once and for all, and to continue to debate this question is pointless and a waste of the group's energy and time. Such discussion leads to divisiveness, polarizations, and judgmental attitudes toward one another for not being "politically correct." Instead, a group can turn attention to identifying what feminist values this group wants to hold as central to what they do together (unity). They then can explore the different ways in which they might work to enact that value, and the different ideas about feminism that each individual can bring to group to actually enrich the group (diversity).

In classrooms or work groups, if the group members spend some time building consensus around a specific value they want to enact to guide their work (see Chapter 3 or 11 for suggestions), they can also explore the wide diversity of perspectives that they bring to being able to act on this value. For example, a work group began experiencing conflict when Linda started bringing to the group's awareness the financial bind that the group was in. The conflict for several months seemed to be focused on anger and resentment at Linda and at one another for either doing or not doing something to create the gloomy financial picture. When the group members explored their unifying value, they realized that they had started out to value the power of responsibility and demystification, and that they still held this as the most important value concerning their finances. Suddenly, Linda, who had been taking the brunt of much of the group's resentment, was recognized as the only one actually behaving in accord with this value. As the group began to explore the various approaches that they each thought the group should take in dealing with the problem, they became aware of many creative and useful ideas that already existed in the group—ideas about solutions that had been obscured by the group's focus on blame and judgment about the "cause" of the problem. Several of the solutions implied ways they could prevent the situation from happening again in the future, approaches that Linda, and others responsible for the finances of the group, had not thought of.

WHEN TRANSFORMATION OF CONFLICT IS NOT POSSIBLE

There are times when it is not possible to transform conflict. In our experience, working toward the ideal for some time is well worth the effort because even when it seems impossible, real movement toward the ideal *is* often possible. Those instances when we have found it not at all possible have one common element—a real lack of commitment on the part of at least one individual within the group to the values that the group has stated openly. Ideally, once values are stated openly, individuals can decide of their own free will whether they wish to continue to work within the group. Sometimes people have limited choices, however, such as in a group of people employed to work together in a business or an institution.

Recognizing that the conflict cannot be transformed in an ideal sense makes it possible for the group to explore what *is* possible in order to create better working relationships. In groups where membership is voluntary, other options include asking for a re-organization of the membership of the group so that those who wish to work effectively together can move forward, or considering ending the group altogether. (See Chapter 10.) Even when these less than ideal circumstances are the best that we can do, individuals can carry with them insights that come from the experience, and build from the experience in their individual and collective futures.

10

Period Pieces

There are things that happen in every group periodically, but not at every gathering. Some of these happenings are pleasant and welcome; others are less pleasant and are unwelcome. In most cases, they are not anticipated and typically not planned for. This can be a source of conflict and frustration. Moving into a new reality requires the best of our creative energies. While we have no "answers," we do offer ideas that have grown from our experience of seeking to stretch our feminist values to address various situations.

PERIODIC REVIEW OF PRINCIPLES OF UNITY

Periodically reviewing Principles of Unity is much like cleaning house—it is something we would often rather not do, but it is necessary and feels good once done! There are no formulas that we have found for identifying when a group's Principles of Unity need to be reviewed. Some groups select a season of the year (we have used winter) as a time for looking over what is being done, and thinking about changes that need to be made. In other groups, the time for taking a new look at the old Principles comes when there is a shift in focus, such as when a task is completed, or when group membership changes.

Reviewing the Principles is vital to the ongoing growth of the group. It is a time for each member to share something of her personal perspective, relating how and why being a part of this group is important to her. As each person brings her own perspective to the work of the group, the group's common interests, hopes, and expectations emerge anew.

Questions that we have found helpful in taking a critical look at our Principles of Unity have been: Are we actually *Doing* what is implied by this Principle? If not, what *are* we doing? What *Principle* is implied in what we *are* doing? For example, in the Friendship Collective, we began with a Principle that we would expect no financial contribution from any member in relation to our work. In practice, we found that there were expenses involved for women who remained a part of the group and that for some women these expenses were a problem. The review of our Principles of Unity made it possible to address these concerns and find a way to state a Principle that brought the tension of financial pressures into the open.

OPEN OR CLOSED GROUPS?

In the ideal, feminist groups usually seek to be inclusive and open to all women who wish to join. In our experience, this is a decision that needs to be carefully considered, because the work of the group and the purpose for which the group exists may not lend itself to open membership. The dilemma becomes, then, how to remain open to new thoughts, to integrating diversity within the group, and yet remain effective in our work.

One way to address this dilemma is to think of openness as relative and changing rather than as an opposing choice of open or closed. There have been times in some of our task-oriented groups when we have needed to maintain stability in our membership in order to meet the pressing demands of tasks that formed our central purpose for gathering. As the demands of the tasks changed, we experienced a natural flow of movement as some women left the group (sometimes temporarily), and others joined.

PEOPLE JOINING AN ONGOING GROUP

In every experience we have had with established groups, integrating new members has always been a welcome, but difficult transition. In relatively open groups, we have found that the demands of constantly integrating new members is a major challenge that requires far more time and energy than we typically expect. Since feminist groups do not "work" like typical groups, women who are new to the group are essentially in a foreign land, in the midst of a new culture that may be totally unfamiliar. The words that are spoken may be that of the predominant culture, but meanings of words take on a new character that existing members often take for granted. Women who have not heard the language of feminist groups find themselves in a muddle trying to figure out what is really going on. Once a group is committed to welcoming new members frequently, existing members need to be constantly aware of these dynamics, and establish ways to ease the transition. At each gathering, time needs to be set aside to explain and clarify what is going on.

Groups that require relative stability in membership may set aside times during the year when the orientation of new members is the only focus for gathering. These events are carefully planned, with each member of the existing group taking responsibility for a portion of the orientation. We have usually included a brief oral history of the group, a review of the Principles of Unity, an orientation to the nature of the work we are doing, and a description of the activities that are expected of all members.

For example, in the Emma Book Store Collective, the ongoing success of running the business depended primarily on each person's ability to staff the store. In addition, we expected everyone to gradually assume other tasks such as ordering new stock, managing the finances, planning for special occasions, working with other groups in the community, and taking care of the physical space. New member potluck dinners were planned four times a year, when those who were interested in joining the collective could gather with us to learn about our history and our Principles of Unity, and to consider what was involved in membership. In the three months following a potluck, new members were expected to participate in each of the major activities of the business with an experienced collective member in order to become oriented to the tasks. In this way, each person had the opportunity to make an informed decision about remaining involved with the group before she made a commitment.

MEMBER LEAVING A GROUP

In groups with unrestricted membership, leaving the group may be a simple matter of not continuing to contribute financially, or not continuing to attend the gatherings. In groups that exist for a purpose that involves personal development, such as a reading group or a consciousness-raising group, the group's purpose may lead to a "live and let live" response to someone leaving: "she simply needs to move on and we all accept that fact."

However, a member leaving the group usually creates a void in the group, therefore, leave-taking needs to be acknowledged openly in some way. In a group where an individual's leaving has consequences for the members of the group, it is especially important to state in the Principles of Unity what the group expects when someone leaves. We have found that creating traditions around this event, similar to the tradition of welcoming new members, is helpful in making this a smooth transition for the group and for the member who is leaving. Since this event represents both an ending and a new beginning, one way to approach it is similar to Closing, with an entire gathering devoted to a Closing relative to the leaving of the individual. Each group member takes the time to express her appreciation, criticism, and affirmation that everyone can carry into their separate futures.

ASKING A MEMBER TO LEAVE A GROUP

As difficult as it may be, there are times when the energies of the group and of an individual are not harmonious. Whatever the problem is, it must be addressed in some constructive way. The assumption that we can "live together happily ever after" is a mythical belief that simply is not consistent with reality. Ending one phase and beginning a new phase is not necessarily a failure; how we deal with one another in terms of personal integrity reveals how well we Do what we Know, and Know what we Do.

When a group finds that one member is not able to function effectively as a group member, the issues must first be addressed openly, bringing to the discussion the fullest of intentions to act in a manner consistent with the group's Principles. All possible avenues for resolving the issues are explored. The discussion continues until every member is certain that the avenue that is chosen is one that is good for the group as well as for the individual.

ENDING A GROUP

Ending a group does not necessarily mean that the group has been a failure. Often it is the celebration of the completion of the purpose for which the group formed. If the purpose was not a specific task that can be wrapped up in a neat package, then knowing when the purpose has been accomplished may not be easily recognizable. For example, a group formed to provide support for one another may find that after a while, women who are in the group have sources of support elsewhere that had not existed when the group was first formed. When this happens, the group may have evolved into something that is no longer meaningful to those involved. When coming to the group's gatherings begins to be more of a chore than a pleasure, it is time to consider ending the group.

Rather than let a group simply fizzle out, we have found that having a specific event around which this is acknowledged—a Closing—provides a means for everyone to close this phase of their experience, taking something from it into the future. Planning for a gathering for a final Closing of the group can be a rich and growthful experience.

11

Classrooms, Committees, and Institutional Constraints

Learning and teaching can take place in the interests of human liberation, even within institutions created for social control.

Kathleen Weiler[1]

When feminist values are brought into a group that exists within patriarchal institutions, they can be a powerful influence toward transformation. This can and does happen by adapting the processes that arise from feminist values. However, we know that the approaches that we have described as "Feminist Process" in this *Handbook* will fail if they are used in a "cookbook" fashion without some agreement by everyone in the group to move toward the value or values that the group as a whole seeks. The methods of Feminist Process can be used as a whole, or adapted, or used in part as a means for moving to new power relations in traditional groups. We caution about creating dogmatic adherence to Feminist Processes without considering the values on which it rests. *Using the approaches of Feminist Process in existing institutions fundamentally depends on the group making a conscious commitment to a value that they freely choose.*

People enter traditional groups such as classrooms and committees expecting that the group will function as usual. When a different way of working together is presented, it is necessary to explain the value basis for making the shift. If the value clearly relates to what the group has already been seeking, then the

89

transition is relatively easy. The group can consider the suggested approaches in their plan toward more fully enacting this value in their meetings.

Classrooms are especially well-steeped in traditions and constrained by institutional rules. Feminist values can be a breath of fresh air in such settings. The traditional teacher–student power imbalance is familiar to everyone who has attended school at any level: the teacher has the power to grade, to offer opinions and judgments, and to speak. The student is institutionally defined as a receiver of grades, a receiver of the teacher's opinions and judgments, and the listener. Overcoming these expectations for roles and behaviors is not easy; some of the institutional expectations cannot be ignored (such as the recording of grades to represent the achievement of a certain curricular or institutional standard).

Two values that we have found to be consistently welcomed by classroom participants are empowerment for all and demystification of content and processes (especially processes for grades). Even though these values could be assumed to be central to what education is all about, they are ironically consistently undermined in most classroom situations. When a teacher brings alternatives to the classroom that clearly enact the values of empowerment for all and demystification of the processes, dramatic change occurs in how "teaching" is done.

While the values of empowerment and demystification are easy to embrace, the actual process of making the shift is a bit of a challenge for everyone. Some people welcome the change, others respond with varying degrees of reserve, and others object at the outset. When individuals who object have a choice (for example, they can enroll in another section of a college course), they are free to leave the group and pursue an alternative. Individuals who are initially hesitant, but willing to stay with the group, frequently relate moving stories about the inner transformations that occur for them during the course of the group's gatherings.[2]

Whoever introduces the new (to the group) process may find it helpful to prepare some written or verbal orientation that is specific to the work of the group, integrating the *value* shift with the *process* shift that is proposed. In classroom situations, the teacher can prepare a course syllabus (with this book as required reading!) in a way that makes the values explicit and reflects how the process will bring those values to life. A member of a committee can prepare a similar description for the group to consider.

The ways in which the ideas of *Peace and Power* influence the work of groups in patriarchal institutions will differ greatly from group to group. The value(s) the group decides to adopt as their guiding principle guides their choice of method. For example, if in a classroom the group decides to work with the value of "sharing" as a focus for their time together, there are many ways this can be done. Leadership can be shared through the rotating role of the Convener, and participation shared through the use of Rotating Chair during discussions. The group may choose a traditional lecture format for course gatherings as an avenue for enacting the value of sharing by the teacher in order to overcome *knowledge* deficits and imbalances. Or, the group can choose to have the teacher lecture for part of the class time, with a Rotating-Chair style of discussion for another part of the time. In addition, the group members can also share drafts of their written work with one another as a way to exchange ideas freely. The possibilities are unlimited.

The key element in making discussions about *what* to do and *how* is clarity about what value the group chooses to embrace. From there, the diversity of ways to enact the value can flow from the group. The group can then periodically examine how well they are doing in creating the value and process changes they are seeking together.

We have found it helpful to take only one value as a starting point in institutional groups. Because most patriarchally defined groups work within traditions that alienate and divide individuals from one another, it is usually not difficult to identify a value from a feminist perspective that appeals to everyone in the group. Most groups, no matter how diverse or disparate in membership, usually have something that they can agree to move toward. Choosing one unifying value provides a focus for the shifts in interaction, and maintains a grounding for times when the confusion of change becomes overwhelming.

The feminist alternative powers, and the commitments in Chapter 3, are the basis for the suggestions in the following sections. The specific suggestions for group shifts in patriarchal institutions arise from having to consider certain constraints imposed by the institution, which usually arise from institutionally defined and sustained power imbalances between individuals. While we describe some of the shifts in terms of individual behaviors, they are built upon fundamental value shifts embraced by the whole group.

Power of Process

Objectives, time frames, and educational structures of evaluation may be used as tools that provide a structure from which to work, but they are not the focal point. The *process* is the important dimension, so that once the interaction begins the structure is *only* a tool and nothing more. *How* the interactions happen becomes the central focus, rather than a precise adherence to a prescribed content. Language is used as a tool to make the process possible, to create mental images that reduce the power imbalances defined by the institution, and to create new relationships. The process itself becomes an important focus for discussion along with the "content" in a classroom, or the "business" of the committee. Priorities related to decision-making shift, so that the urgency of making decisions lessens and the group learns to value the wisdom that comes with the Process. When this value is primary, Closing can be a powerful approach to learning to enact this value.

Power of Letting Go

All participants let go of old habits and behaviors in order to make room for personal and collective growth. Teachers and committee chairs let go of "power-over" attitudes and ways of being; students and members let go of "tell me what to do" attitudes and ways of being. All participants move into ways of being that are personally empowering and that also nurture the empowerment of others. All participants share their ideas, but shift to a focus of fully hearing and understanding others' points of view.

Power of the Whole

Mutual help networks within the group are encouraged. Every individual is responsible for investing talents and skills for the interests of the group as a whole. Each participant, whether teacher or student, leader or member, is accountable to the *whole group* for negotiating specific agendas, keeping the group informed about absences, leaving early, arriving late, or initiating particular activities within the group.

Power of Collectivity

Each participant is taken into account in the group's planning-in-process. The group works to address the needs of those who are moving into individual journeys where others may not be going. The needs of those who are having specific struggles are addressed by the group in some way. Individuals do not compete with one another; rather, the needs of all are acknowledged and addressed as equally valuable. Every decision is made with full understanding of every point of view within the group.

Power of Unity

Unity is recognized as coming from the expression of differing points of view so that they can be understood, and integrated into a richer and fuller appreciation of every individual. Out of this appreciation, each individual participates in clarifying the principle(s) that the group has come to embrace. By actively seeking to understand differing perspectives that each person brings, the group members can reach a fuller understanding of what unifies them. This provides a strong basis for transforming conflict.

Power of Sharing

All participants enter the group with talents, skills, and abilities related to the work of the group, and actively engage in sharing their individual talents. Leaders and teachers enter groups with previously developed capabilities that are shared according to the needs of the group and in consideration of the structure-as-tool. Members and students enter the group with personal talents, background, and experiences that are valued and shared. All participants enter the group open to what others can share and open to learning from every other member.

Power of Integration

All dimensions of the situation are acknowledged in planning for the experience. Each individual's unique and self-defined needs for the experience are acknowledged and integrated into the process. The first portion of each gathering is used as a time for each individual to express their priorities, needs, and wishes for the gathering so that these can be integrated as a part of the process for that gathering.

Power of Nurturing

Each participant is respected fully and unconditionally, and regarded as necessary and integral to the experience of the group. Tasks, activities, and approaches are planned to nurture the gradual growth of new skills and abilities, assuring that *every* participant can be successful both in terms of the goals of the group, and in terms of individual needs.

Power of Distribution

Resources required for the work of the group (information, books, funds, space, transportation, equipment) are made equally available and accessible to all members of the group. Resources that might be purchased by individual members (such as books, equipment, transportation) are shared (for example, through libraries, laboratories, resource rooms, or sharing among members), so that any individual who chooses not to use personal resources in this way, or who cannot, has equal access to the material. Issues arising from material inequalities among members are addressed openly to expose and overcome power imbalances perpetuated by economic privilege or disadvantage.

Power of Intuition

The process that occurs, and the nature of what is addressed in the group, depend as much on the experience of the moment as on any other factor. What emerges as important for the group to address in the moment is what happens. Letting go of what "ought" to happen is valued as a new skill that makes possible what *will* happen.

Power of Consciousness

Ethical dimensions of the process are valued as fundamental to the goals and purposes assigned to the group by the institution. Every decision is considered in terms of its ethical dimensions. A portion of each gathering devoted to a Closing—Appreciation, Criticism, and Affirmation—is one way to move to group awareness of the values represented in what is done.

Power of Diversity

Deliberate processes are planned and enacted to integrate points of view of individuals and groups whose perspectives are usually not addressed. The experiences (through writings, personal encounters, poetry, song, drama, and so on) of minority groups, of different classes, of third world people, of women, are given a deliberate focus in relation to whatever the group is addressing. Rotating Chair is one way to assure that every voice is heard in a group, so that the diversity that exists within the group can be expressed.

Power of Responsibility

All participants assume full responsibility as the agent for their role in the process. Rotating Conveners is one way to nurture leadership. Rotating Chair assures that everyone has a way to assume responsibility for what happens in group meetings. Each individual assumes responsibility to demystify the processes involved in all activities, so that each member of the group has equal access to participating and understanding what is going on. In classrooms, "grades" are viewed as each individual's responsibility; they are viewed as a tool to represent what the individual earns through demonstrated accomplishments. The teacher, like leaders in other types of groups, has a special responsibility to help demystify the workings of the institution, and to make explicit the political process within the institution.

Taking steps to adapt Feminist Process in patriarchal institutions can be risky, frightening, and discouraging. There are failures, and sometimes groups seem unable to move beyond mere token acts of working in ways that are envisioned here. Often the hoped-for benefits and changes that happen seem completely invisible, only to become visible long after the group has ended. An important step that can be taken to overcome the isolation, fear, and frustration is to create a reality outside of the institution where feminist values can be enacted more fully within a group or groups committed to creating liberating transformations for all people. Experiencing a community, even though it may be a small group, where the ideals can be more fully realized, provides a place of centering, of concentrating our energies in a healing direction, of support for the values we are seeking to enact, and for exploring more fully what might be possible. Then, when the disappointments of the old world come crashing in, the visions of the new possibilities are there . . . somewhere.

Notes

ACKNOWLEDGMENTS

1. Margaretdaughters, Inc., was created in 1984 by Charlene Eldridge Wheeler and Peggy L. Chinn. The name was a tribute to our Mothers, Margaret Eldridge and Margaret Tatum, who taught us the importance of Doing what we Know. We published feminist writing, calendars, and provided workshops on the use of *Peace and Power* until 1989 when we terminated our publishing adventure, joining a large and respectable number of other small feminist presses that also succumbed to the realities of the publishing world.

PROLOGUE

1. Anne Cameron, *Daughters of Copper Woman* (Press Gang Publishers, 603 Powell Street, Vancouver, British Columbia, 1981, p. 53.) Through the ancient myths of the native women of Vancouver Island, Anne Cameron offers "a shining vision of womanhood, of how the spiritual and social power of women—though relentlessly challenged—can Endure and Survive." (From the back cover.) In the Preface, Cameron states: "From these few women [the native women of Vancouver Island who told her the stories], with the help of a collective of women, to all other women, with love, and in Sisterhood, this leap of faith that the mistakes and abuse of the past need not continue. There is a better way of doing things. Some of us remember that better way."
2. Anne Cameron, *ibid.,* p. 63.
3. Barbara Walker in *The Crone* (San Francisco: Harper & Row, 1985) has contributed another major work that explores the past roles of

97

female elders and draws on carefully researched historical material to bring her clearly focused insights to current events in women's lives.

4. Mary Daly uses hyphens like this to convey a new possibility within the word, in this case meaning putting back together the pieces, the "members," of what we Know as women. Her books *Gyn/Ecology* and the *Wickedary* provide more enlightening study on her work with language and word usage (see Note 5, Chapter 2).

5. Diane Stein, *All Women Are Healers: A Comprehensive Guide to Natural Healing* (Freedom, CA: Crossing Press, 1980), while primarily an exploration of the various paths to natural healing, Diane looks at women's roles and contributions to healing. She weaves throughout her writing rich historical evidence, combined with well-informed speculation about the origins of healing as women's art.

6. One of the most important books of this wave of feminism addresses the consistent and persistent erasure of women's knowledge and women's writing. In *Women of Ideas and What Men Have Done to Them* (Boston: Routledge & Kegan Paul, 1982), Dale Spender analyzes over three centuries of women's writing. She concludes: "We are women producing knowledge which is often different from that produced by men, in a society controlled by men. If they like what we produce they will appropriate it, if they can use what we produce (even against us) they will take it, if they do not want to know, they will lose it. But rarely, if ever, will they treat it as they treat their own" (p. 9). For several years, this book was out of print and very difficult to find; causing us to wonder if the very thing Dale Spender warned us of was happening to her own work. Most fortunately, this title has been released by Pandora Press, London and Cambridge, MA, 1988.

7. During the all too brief time we were allowed with Wilma Scott Heide, she shared gems with us that remain part of our thinking still. One day during a conversation, we were sharing the information about the word "testify" that is in Barbara G. Walker's *The Woman's Encyclopedia of Myths and Secrets* (New York: Harper & Row, 1983), pp. 793–794. Since the derivation of the term relies on certain genetically determined gender parts, the term "testify" was deemed by Wilma as inappropriate for women to use. She suggested that we use the term "breastify" to indicate our truth-telling.

8. We are very grateful to all of the women who shared their thoughts about the creation of a Do-able peace list and are particularly indebted to the following: Connie Blair, Loraine Guyette, and other doctoral students (University of Colorado, School of Nursing, spring

1991), Pat Hickson, Janet Quinn, Carole Schroeder and her children Ben and Morgan, and Christine Tanner.

CHAPTER 1

1. Frances Moore Lappé, *Diet for a Small Planet: Tenth Anniversary Edition* (New York: Ballantine Books, 1990), p. 15.
2. From "The Rock Will Wear Away" by Meg Christian and Holly Near; performed by Meg Christian on the album *Face the Music* produced by Olivia Records, Box 70237, Los Angeles, CA 90070, 1977. On the album insert, Meg writes: "The theme of the chorus [quoted here] is a common one: many small, weak entities joining together to defeat a larger, stronger one. Holly heard the rock-water imagery in a Vietnamese poem, while I fondly recall the flies in the elephant's nose in Judy Grahn's poem. You haven't really heard this song until you've sung it yourself with a whole roomful of women. For me, that experience is one of those moments when I feel our growing collective strength and purpose . . ."
3. Our definition of "praxis" is adapted from *Pedagogy of the Oppressed* by Paulo Friere (New York: The Seabury Press, 1970), p. 36.
4. In *A Passion for Friends: Toward a Philosophy of Female Affection* (Boston: Beacon Press, 1986), Janice Raymond provides a landmark vision of Gyn/affection, the ability to be moved by, and to deeply move other women. This profound experience of female friendship, formed in the cultural commitments that women make to their Selves and each other, is the grounding for women's personal and political empowerment.
5. A comprehensive exploration of a feminist concept of "empowerment" is in the premier issue of *Woman of Power: A Magazine of Feminism, Spirituality, and Politics,* spring 1984. The journal is published quarterly by Woman of Power, Inc., P.O. Box 827, Cambridge, MA 02238.
6. Awareness is a central theme of feminist literature. In *The Politics of Reality: Essays in Feminist Theory* (Freedom, CA: Crossing Press, 1983), Marilyn Frye explores a wide range of fundamental issues including oppression, sexism, and racism. In her essay titled "Lesbian Feminism and the Gay Rights Movement: Another View of Male Supremacy, Another Separatism" she states: "One of the privileges of being normal and ordinary is a certain unconsciousness. When one is that which is taken as the norm in one's social environment, one does not have to think about it . . . if one is marginal, one does not have the privilege of not noticing what one is. This absence of privilege is a presence of knowledge" (p. 146).

7. A classic collection of feminist writings from the women's movement of the late 1960s and early 1970s is available in *Radical Feminism* edited by Anne Koedt, Ellen Levine, and Anita Rapone (New York: Quadrangle, 1973). In the essay "The Tyranny of Structurelessness," Joreen examines the informal elite patterns of decision making that exist in structured and unstructured groups, and the essential elements of "democratic structuring" necessary to achieve healthy functioning within a group. These elements include: delegation by the group, responsibility to the group, distribution of authority, rotation of tasks along rational criteria, diffusion of information, and equal access to resources. Our concept of consensus builds on and expands these concepts.

8. In *Pure Lust: Elemental Feminist Philosophy* (Boston: Beacon Press, 1984), Mary Daly states: "Although friendship is not possible among all feminists, the work of Be-Friending can be shared by all, and all can benefit from the Metamorphospheric activity. Be-Friending involves Weaving a context in which women can Realize our Self-Transforming, metapatterning participation in Be-ing. Therefore it implies the creation of an atmosphere in which women are enabled to be friends. Every woman who contributes to the creation of this atmosphere functions as a catalyst for the evolution of other women and for the forming and unfolding of genuine friendships" (p. 374).

CHAPTER 2

1. Notes from an Interview on "Womanpower" with Joanna Rogers Macy in *Woman of Power,* spring 1984, p. 12. Joanna Rogers Macy is co-founder of Interhelp (P.O. Box 331, Northampton, MA 01060), an international organization that provides workshops on "Despair and Empowerment in the Nuclear Age." Bobbi Levi, who leads these workshops in Massachusetts, provided this interview for *Woman of Power.*

2. Notes from an Interview on "Womanpower" with Diane Mariechild in *Woman of Power,* spring 1984, p. 18. Diane Mariechild is a mother, teacher, healer, and author of *Motherwit: A Feminist Guide to Psychic Development* (Freedom, CA: Crossing Press, 1981).

3. Grace Rowan, "Looking for a New Model of Power." *Woman of Power,* spring 1984, p. 67. She is described in this issue as "the co-founder of a shelter for battered women. She sees herself as a woman with power, and uses this power in her practice as a psychologist and for healing. She is a wise old woman on a journey to wholeness."

4. Power as defined in patriarchal terms, is the capacity to impose one's will on others, accompanied by a willingness to apply negative sanctions against those who oppose that will. This translates into a "love

of power," where the fact of *having* the power becomes more important, more critical, than *what* that power is used for or what results from the use of that power. Any measure that is necessary to retain that power is considered justifiable. Further, individuals who are being manipulated or controlled do not recognize these underlying dynamics, because we are so thoroughly taught that the power structure, as it is set up, is the "only way."

5. Our model of patriarchal power and feminist alternatives was originally published in *Cassandra: Radical Feminist Nurses NewsJournal* Vol. 2, No. 2, May 1984, p. 10. In developing these ideas, we also used *The Aquarian Conspiracy: Personal and Social Transformation in the 1980's* by Marilyn Ferguson (Los Angeles: J.P. Tarcher, Inc., 1980) as a point of reference. Ferguson does not identify the prevailing power model as "patriarchal," but she does contrast that model with transforming power modes emerging today. We borrowed a few of her names for various forms of power, but where we did so we conceptualized them from our own feminist frame of reference.

Nancy Greenleaf provided the insights and suggestions that led to our inclusion in this edition of the patriarchal Power of Accumulation and the Feminist Alternative Power of Distribution. In a letter dated February 7, 1989, after reviewing a near-final draft of the manuscript, Nancy wrote: "I found myself wanting to add to your power model . . . something that addresses the power of the 'free market'; a godlike 'invisible hand' that sorts the worthy from the undeserving and assumes 'self-interest' as a primary motivational force. This notion of power is inextricably combined with patriarchal notions, but it specifically addresses material (economic) well-being. The feminist alternative is the power that accrues through material sharing—of food—of land or space and the de-emphasis on privatization of property. The feminist alternative would mean a commitment to bear witness to and expose material inequality."

We named and described the feminist alternatives from a wide range of feminist theory, as well as our own experiences working in feminist groups. It is impossible to list here all the sources that influenced the creation of this model; however, in addition to the sources cited in Chapter 1, the following sources have been particularly important to us:

Louise Bernikow, *Among Women*. New York: Harmony Books, 1980.
Charlotte Bunch, *Passionate Politics: Feminist Theory in Action*. New York: St. Martin's Press, 1987.

Mary Daly, Gyn/Ecology: *The Metaethics of Radical Feminism,* 1978; *Pure Lust: Elemental Feminist Philosophy,* 1984; and *Websters' First New Intergalactic Wickedary of the English Language* (in cahoots with Jane Caputi), 1987. All titles published by Beacon Press, Boston, MA.

Andrea Dworkin, *Right-Wing Women.* New York: Perigee Books, 1983.

Riane Eisler, *The Chalice and the Blade.* San Francisco: Harper & Row, 1987.

Susan Griffin, *Woman and Nature: The Roaring Inside Her.* New York: Harper Colophon Books, 1978.

Sarah Lucia Hoagland, *Lesbian Ethics: Toward New Value.* Palo Alto: Institute of Lesbian Studies, 1988.

Bell Hooks, *Feminist Theory: From Margin to Center.* Boston: South End Press, 1984.

Pam McAllister, (Ed.): *Reweaving the Web of Life: Feminism and Non-violence.* Philadelphia: New Society Publisher, 1982.

Kate Millett, *Sexual Politics.* New York: Avon Books, 1969.

Cherrie Moraga, and Gloria Anzaldua (Eds.): *This Bridge Called My Back:* Writings by Radical Women of Color. Watertown, MA: Persephone Press, 1981.

Robin Morgan, (Ed.): *Sisterhood is Powerful: An Anthology of Writings from the Women's Liberation Movement.* New York: Vintage Books, 1970.

Nel Noddings, *Women and Evil.* Berkeley: University of California Press, 1989.

Adrienne Rich, *On Lies, Secrets and Silence: Selected Prose 1966–1978.* New York: W.W. Norton, 1979.

Anne Wilson Schaef, *When Society Becomes an Addict.* San Francisco: Harper & Row, 1987.

CHAPTER 4

1. Margo Adair, *Working Inside Out: Tools for Change.* Berkeley: Wingbow Press, 1984, p. 284. This is a powerful, healing book that provides useful tools for bringing together the personal, spiritual, and political aspects of our lives, individually and collectively.

2. Kathleen MacPherson first identified four components around which the Menopause Collective formed their Principles of Unity. Her experience is related in her doctoral dissertation, completed in 1986 at Brandeis University, titled "Feminist Praxis in the Making: The Menopause Collective." The components we present here draw on Kathleen's ideas, as well as the ideas and experience of the Friendship

Collective, where we have worked extensively to develop Principles of Unity as our basis.

3. For more information about the early work of the Friendship Collective, see: "Just Between Friends: AJN Friendship Survey" (November 1987, pp. 1456–1458) and "Friends on Friendship," *American Journal of Nursing* (August 1988), pp. 1094–1096.

CHAPTER 5

1. We have participated in groups that range from 6 to 36 in number. In groups smaller than 6, it is easy to "skip" the process and slide into a more social interaction. In groups as large as 36, the process has provided a sense of being in a group of "ideal" size, where every participant has a feeling of being included and fully participating. We do not yet know what the limits of group size might be.

2. In *Pure Lust* (Boston: Beacon Press, 1984), Mary Daly states: "First of all, Gnomic Nags should note that Real Presence implies being pre-sentient—'feeling or perceiving beforehand.' . . . When women are Present to our Selves, . . . to be presentient is to be animated with hope. This presentient Presence is Positively Powerful, for it implies our capacity to presentiate, that is 'to make or render present in place or time; to cause to be perceived or realized as present' (O.E.D.). Real Presence of the Self, then, which is participation in Powers of Be-ing, implies powers to Realize as present our past and future Selves" (pp. 147–148).

3. Susan Cady, Marian Ronan, and Hal Taussig, *SOPHIA: The Future of Feminist Spirituality* (San Francisco: Harper & Row, 1986).

CHAPTER 6

1. We appreciate Anne Montes for suggesting the idea and for sharing her insights for Random Ravings.

CHAPTER 8

1. We are grateful to Gracie Lyons, who presented this guideline in her book *Constructive Criticism: A Handbook,* published by the Issues in Radical Therapy Collective, Berkeley, CA, 1976. We have used this book as a source for developing constructive criticism in several contexts. Unfortunately, we have not been able to locate the collective or a source for obtaining the book since 1979. Gracie's approach is based on Marxist/Maoist theory. Our approach draws on hers but comes from a feminist frame of reference.

2. Margo Adair, *Working Inside Out: Tools for Change* (Berkeley: Wingbow Press, 1984). For specific information on how to use affirmations in your personal life to create change, see Chapter 3, "Creating a Language to Speak to Your Deeper Self."

3. Notice that these questions are drawn directly from Peace, the intent with which we enter the process. See Chapter 1.

4. In an article titled "With Gossip Aforethought" in the first issue of *Gossip: A Journal of Lesbian Feminist Ethics,* Anna Livia explains the importance of naming the agent and the source of information to build trust, especially when verbal stories we tell one another are our primary, if not only, way to find out what we need to know to work together. "It is reasonable to ask where a particular piece of gossip comes from. If a lesbian refuses to say, it is ostensibly to protect herself and her source. Why does she need protection, and from whom, if she repeats truthfully what she believes to be the truth? . . . If you won't say how you know [about a person or situation], are we to think you made it up yourself?" (p. 62). Gossip is published by Onlywomen Press, Ltd., 38 Mount Pleasant, London WC1X OAP.

5. We appreciate Elizabeth Berrey for creating and owning this as her affirmation in the Friendship Collective. It is a statement that reflects what she has meant to us, over and over again, in the work that we do and how we live our lives.

CHAPTER 9

1. It is sometimes instructional to browse the dictionary for definitions of words, as much for what the words have come to mean in popular usage, but additionally for the convoluted and interrelated shades of meanings attached to them. For instance, in *Webster's New Collegiate* dictionary the definitions of conflict speak to "competitive or opposing action of incompatibles"; "hostile encounter." *The American Heritage Dictionary* starts right out with "a prolonged battle, a controversy; disagreement; opposition" and goes on to clarify the differences between conflict and contest (apparently the degree of force involved makes a difference!). Going on to look up "hostile" we encounter words like "enemy, enmity, not hospitable, unfriendly." Little wonder that we find conflict difficult to embrace as a potentially growth producing experience!

2. Suzette Haden Elgin has written a number of books dealing with the *Gentle Art of Verbal Self-Defense,* ranging from *More on . . .* to *The Last Word On . . . Staying Well With . . .* and *Success With . . .* All of them are excellent and full of information about her approach to

the modes of communication and ways to break nasty loops. The techniques she recommends and the responses outlined are manageable and readily learned for incorporating into your everyday life.

3. In Dale Spender's *Man-Made Language* (2nd ed., Pandora Press, London and Cambridge, MA, 1985), she includes a poem at the beginning that starts with the line:

   "what men dub tattle gossip women's talk
   is really revolutionary activity . . ."

   She goes on to note ". . . we will have to invest the language with our own authentic meanings, and repudiate many of those which are currently accented as accurate . . ." (p. 5).

4. Mary Daly in Cahoots with Jane Caputi, *Websters' First Intergalactic Wickedary of the English Language* (Boston: Beacon Press, 1987), have a lively discussion of "Gossip" both as noun and as verb in Word-Web Two.

5. Peggy L. Chinn, "Gossip: A Transformative Art for Nursing Education in the *Journal of Nursing Education* 29:7 (September 1990), pp. 318–321.

6. A book that we have found particularly helpful is *The Dance of Anger* by Harriet Goldhor Lerner. It is a book written especially for women who have learned to fear anger; the approaches to dealing with anger are safe, constructive and, most of all, achievable. She provides useful and practical guidelines for changing interactions so that everyone involved benefits.

CHAPTER 11

1. Kathleen Weiler, *Women Teaching for Change: Gender, Class & Power* (Massachusetts: Bergin & Garvey Publishers, Inc., South Hadley, MA, 1988), p. 152.

2. For example, registrants have stated:

   "Wasn't sure what I expected, but I came away feeling like I have an openness for exchange of ideas. I now have difficulty conceptualizing a theory class "taught" (convened, please) apart from feminist process. Keep this format, please!"

   "It took me a while to become accustomed to the course format. But I enjoyed it. It was very stimulating."

   "At first I wasn't certain about the different format of class sessions. But I have never experienced discussion so enriching. I have never enjoyed writing a paper before. This time I did."

About the Authors

Charlene Eldridge Wheeler, MS, RN, provides independent workshops for groups of women and nurses who gather to learn the approaches described in this book, and for purposes of self-healing and support. She is also reclaiming her first vocation as an artist, focusing on fiber arts. Her nursing practice has been in the areas of Public Health Nursing and Substance Abuse Treatment programs. She has published journal articles on communications, nursing administration, nursing history, and feminism.

Peggy L. Chinn, PhD, RN, FAAN, is professor of nursing at the University of Colorado Health Sciences Center School of Nursing in Denver, Colorado. She is the founding editor of *Advances in Nursing Science.* Her nursing practice has been in the areas of Child Health and Women's Health. She has published books and journal articles on child health, nursing theory development, nursing education, and feminism.

Date Due

BRODART, CO.   Cat. No. 23-233-003   Printed in U.S.A.